MACMILLAN MASTER GUIDES

GENERAL EDITOR: JAMES GIBSON

JANE AUSTEN	*Emma* Norman Page
	Sense and Sensibility Judy Simons
	Persuasion Judy Simons
	Pride and Prejudice Raymond Wilson
	Mansfield Park Richard Wirdnam
SAMUEL BECKETT	*Waiting for Godot* Jennifer Birkett
WILLIAM BLAKE	*Songs of Innocence and Songs of Experience* Alan Tomlinson
ROBERT BOLT	*A Man for All Seasons* Leonard Smith
CHARLOTTE BRONTË	*Jane Eyre* Robert Miles
EMILY BRONTË	*Wuthering Heights* Hilda D. Spear
JOHN BUNYAN	*The Pilgrim's Progress* Beatrice Batson
GEOFFREY CHAUCER	*The Miller's Tale* Michael Alexander
	The Pardoner's Tale Geoffrey Lester
	The Wife of Bath's Tale Nicholas Marsh
	The Knight's Tale Anne Samson
	The Prologue to the Canterbury Tales Nigel Thomas and Richard Swan
JOSEPH CONRAD	*The Secret Agent* Andrew Mayne
CHARLES DICKENS	*Bleak House* Dennis Butts
	Great Expectations Dennis Butts
	Hard Times Norman Page
GEORGE ELIOT	*Middlemarch* Graham Handley
	Silas Marner Graham Handley
	The Mill on the Floss Helen Wheeler
T. S. ELIOT	*Selected Poems* Andrew Swarbrick
HENRY FIELDING	*Joseph Andrews* Trevor Johnson
E. M. FORSTER	*A Passage to India* Hilda D. Spear
	Howards End Ian Milligan
WILLIAM GOLDING	*The Spire* Rosemary Sumner
	Lord of the Flies Raymond Wilson
OLIVER GOLDSMITH	*She Stoops to Conquer* Paul Ranger
THOMAS HARDY	*The Mayor of Casterbridge* Ray Evans
	Tess of the d'Urbervilles James Gibson
	Far from the Madding Crowd Colin Temblett-Wood
BEN JONSON	*Volpone* Michael Stout
JOHN KEATS	*Selected Poems* John Garrett
RUDYARD KIPLING	*Kim* Leonée Ormond
PHILIP LARKIN	*The Whitsun Weddings* and *The Less Deceived* Andrew Swarbrick
D.H. LAWRENCE	*Sons and Lovers* R. P. Draper

MACMILLAN MASTER GUIDES

HARPER LEE	*To Kill a Mockingbird* Jean Armstrong
GERARD MANLEY HOPKINS	*Selected Poems* R. J. C. Watt
CHRISTOPHER MARLOWE	*Doctor Faustus* David A. Male
THE METAPHYSICAL POETS	Joan van Emden
THOMAS MIDDLETON and WILLIAM ROWLEY	*The Changeling* Tony Bromham
ARTHUR MILLER	*The Crucible* Leonard Smith *Death of a Salesman* Peter Spalding
GEORGE ORWELL	*Animal Farm* Jean Armstrong
WILLIAM SHAKESPEARE	*Richard II* Charles Barber *Othello* Tony Bromham *Hamlet* Jean Brooks *King Lear* Francis Casey *Henry V* Peter Davison *The Winter's Tale* Diana Devlin *Julius Caesar* David Elloway *Macbeth* David Elloway *The Merchant of Venice* A. M. Kinghorn *Measure for Measure* Mark Lilly *Henry IV Part I* Helen Morris *Romeo and Juliet* Helen Morris *A Midsummer Night's Dream* Kenneth Pickering *The Tempest* Kenneth Pickering *Coriolanus* Gordon Williams *Antony and Cleopatra* Martin Wine *Twelfth Night* R. P. Draper
RICHARD SHERIDAN	*The School for Scandal* Paul Ranger *The Rivals* Jeremy Rowe
ALFRED TENNYSON	*In Memoriam* Richard Gill
EDWARD THOMAS	*Selected Poems* Gerald Roberts
ANTHONY TROLLOPE	*Barchester Towers* K. M. Newton
JOHN WEBSTER	*The White Devil* and *The Duchess of Malfi* David A. Male
VIRGINIA WOOLF	*To the Lighthouse* John Mepham *Mrs Dalloway* Julian Pattison
WILLIAM WORDSWORTH	*The Prelude Books I and II* Helen Wheeler

MACMILLAN MASTER GUIDES

SELECTED POEMS OF

EDWARD THOMAS

GERALD ROBERTS

MACMILLAN

First published 1988 by
MACMILLAN PRESS LTD
Houndmills, Basingstoke, Hampshire RG21 6XS
and London
Companies and representatives
throughout the world

ISBN 0–333–44263–6

A catalogue record for this book is available
from the British Library.

This book is printed on paper suitable for recycling and
made from fully managed and sustained forest sources.

10   9   8   7   6   5   4   3   2
05   04   03   02   01   00   99   98

Printed in Malaysia

CONTENTS

GENERAL EDITOR'S PREFACE

The aim of the Macmillan Master Guides is to help you to appreciate the book you are studying by providing information about it and by suggesting ways of reading and thinking about it which will lead to a fuller understanding. The section on the writer's life and background has been designed to illustrate those aspects of the writer's life which have influenced the work, and to place it in its personal and literary context. The summaries and critical commentary are of special importance in that each brief summary of the action is followed by an examination of the significant critical points. The space which might have been given to repetitive explanatory notes has been devoted to a detailed analysis of the kind of passage which might confront you in an examination. Literary criticism is concerned with both the broader aspects of the work being studied and with its detail. The ideas which meet us in reading a great work of literature, and their relevance to us today, are an essential part of our study, and our Guides look at the thought of their subject in some detail. But just as essential is the craft with which the writer has constructed his work of art, and this may be considered under several technical headings — characterisation, language, style and stagecraft, for example.

The authors of these Guides are all teachers and writers of wide experience, and they have chosen to write about books they admire and know well in the belief that they can communicate their admiration to you. But you yourself must read and know intimately the book you are studying. No one can do that for you. You should see this book as a lamp-post. Use it to shed light, not to lean against. If you know your text and know what it is saying about life, and how it says it, then you will enjoy it, and there is no better way of passing an examination in literature.

JAMES GIBSON

ACKNOWLEDGEMENTS

Note on the text used. With ten exceptions, all the poems discussed in the following commentary appear in *Selected Poems of Edward Thomas* edited by R. S. Thomas (Faber & Faber, 1964). The additional poems may be found in any of the standard complete editions of Thomas, for example by Edna Longley (Collins, 1973), or by R. G. Thomas (Oxford University Press, 1978). The latter shows some textual differences from earlier editions.

In preparing this guide, the author has found particularly valuable the editions of Thomas's poems by Edna Longley and R. G. Thomas, as well as the biography of the poet by Professor Thomas (full details are given in 'Further Reading').

The author would also like to thank the staff of the British Library in Bloomsbury and the Senate House Library, University of London, for their assistance.

GERALD ROBERTS

Cover illustration: *A Day in Late Autumn* by E. W. Waite, by courtesy of the Bridgeman Art Library.

1 INTRODUCTION

> If I could really bring these things pure and clear through verse into people's heads it would be a great thing. Well, I don't know either and I am not sure that I care. I am not trying to do anything in particular but only hoping that at least I have stepped into the nearest approach I ever made yet to self-expression. (Edward Thomas to Eleanor Farjeon, *The Last Four Years*, p. 146)

After many, often frustrating years of prose-writing, Edward Thomas came to realise that his ideal as an author was not the imitation of revered literary models, the painstaking construction of purple passages of elegant prose, but finding and expressing himself as he really was. This realisation was a shattering one, for it meant recognising that serious literature depended not on 'mannerism' and style, but on the reality for the writer of the experience which he interpreted, and hence necessarily the interest and significance of the writer's own personality.

In his journey to this discovery Thomas can be seen, in his critical and biographical writing around 1910–12, arriving at a rejection of the doctrine of words for words' sake. The poet, Algernon Swinburne, he remarked, seemed to write 'for the sake of constructing formally perfect and sonorous sentences', the exotic Lafcadio Hearn, who wrote several books on Japan, played 'games of skill with words', while the 'hard and inhuman . . . marble' of Walter Pater's style inspired Thomas to comment that 'literature is not for connoisseurs'.

This growing desire for artistic liberation expressed itself in a change of literary form, and it was in verse that Thomas found himself, both as a man and a writer. He produced the 140 or so poems that make up his total output in the period extending from December 1914 to January 1917. There had, of course, been juvenilia, and there was a pseudo-translation from the Welsh that he slipped into his *Beautiful Wales* (1909), but these do not detract from the substantially correct picture of a man to whom poetry came in a rush.

There is a staggering disproportion between this comparatively slim collection of verse and half a lifetime of prose: he wrote some 40 prose works, topographical, critical and biographical, not to speak of an estimated million and more words of reviews. Some of the prose is now being re-published, and *The South Country* and *Richard Jefferies* in particular are evidence of the fineness and sensitivity of his writing, but it seems clear that, barring some radical revision of literary taste, the poetry will continue to be the foundation of his reputation.

Only twenty of these poems appeared in print before his death at the beginning of the Battle of Arras in April 1917, and although all his work appeared within twelve months after, it attracted, and continued to attract only a limited number of readers for the next thirty years. In the fifties, a remarkable change of fortune began, as his reputation started to emerge from the shadow-land of minor poetry and the quaint atmosphere of Georgianism into the full light of critical (and popular) approval. Within twenty years he was being greeted, on the one hand, as 'one of the most profound poets of the century' (C. H. Sisson, *English Poetry*, 1971), and at the same time as 'one of the most popular of twentieth-century poets' (W. Cooke, *Edward Thomas*, 1970).

There is an interesting comparison here with the fortunes of the Jesuit poet Gerard Manley Hopkins. Hopkins's poetry was hardly known at his death in 1889, and even after the first edition prepared by Robert Bridges in 1918, interest in his work remained confined to a few discriminating readers. Yet, after the second edition in 1930, Hopkins was hailed by critics and poets, as well as by the general literary reader, as someone who offered a poetry for the times, inspiring and disturbing in content, original and individual in utterance. As has to some extent happened to Thomas, Hopkins was transformed into a 'modern' poet, with his own influence and followers.

He and Thomas shared too a love of nature and a desire to express their almost inexpressible response to the natural world in a language sensitive to the rhythms of the speaking voice. Both were men whose poetry breathes sincerity and individuality, and it is on this final point that the reader may be left to the following pages. Thomas wrote about his hero, the Wiltshire man and nature-writer, Richard Jefferies, that he described the English countryside 'because he could not uncover his own soul without it'. Thomas's exploration of the outside world is also an exploration and revelation of self, and the style in which it is done reflects the man. In the words he used about Jefferies, it is true to say that there is no style 'which so rapidly convinces the reader of its source in the heart of one of the sincerest of men'.

2 LIFE AND WRITING

> The subject of this book was a man who was continually writing about himself, whether openly or in disguise. He was by nature inclined to thinking about himself and when he came to write he naturally wrote about himself. (Edward Thomas, *George Borrow*, London 1912, p. 1.)

At first sight, Philip Edward Thomas's love of the countryside seems surprising in one who was born (3 March 1879) between Wandsworth and Clapham Commons and spent his youth in these and adjacent areas of South London. But in these places, by walks into the still existing woods and fields to the south as well as over Wimbledon Common, and on holidays in Swindon and South Wales, it was possible to observe and enjoy the countryside and wildlife which he described in the *Childhood of Edward Thomas* and recorded in the diary that appeared in his first book, *The Woodland Life*.

Thomas's parents both came from Wales, while the name Eastaway, which he later adopted as a pseudonym, was that of a family connection in the Bristol Channel area. Although one step removed from the country, his Welshness was no paper matter, and he was to show his affection for things Welsh – or at least South Welsh – by his frequent visits there, his Welsh acquaintances, and the regular use of Wales in his writing. Essays like 'Penderyn', 'Mother and Son', and 'At a Cottage Door' reflect concern at the erosion of rural life, as well as fascination with such typical Thomas paradoxes as the 'ugly–beautiful' town of Swansea.

He went to school at Battersea Grammar and St Paul's, where he intermittently showed he was clever, but on the whole had a lonely and sometimes unhappy time. The eldest of six brothers, he was the one on whom his father, who worked in the Board of Trade, placed his particular ambitions, intending that he should make a successful career in the Civil Service. But from an early age Edward had determined to be a writer, and with the encouragement of a neighbour, the journalist James Ashcroft Noble, he was, by the age of 16, publishing nature articles in London periodicals. In the essay 'How I Began' in *The Last Sheaf*, Thomas regretted the influence on his early writing of convention and authority: 'I virtually neglected in my writing the feelings that belonged to my own nature and my own times of life.' This (retrospective) regret at a failing in sincerity was also accompanied, in later life, by a sense of the disparity between the language of his prose and a more natural form of expression, closer to that of speech. Through his poetry he solved the first problem completely, and came as close as perhaps he wished to closing the gap in his use of language.

In 1894 he and James Noble's daughter, Helen, became acquainted, and soon fell in love. Their first Utopian intentions were to have a secret physical relationship without marriage, but circumstances (including pregnancy) forced them to change their plans. The story is beautifully told in Helen's memoir of her life with Edward, *As It Was* (1926) and *World Without End* (1931). Combined with R. G. Thomas's probably definitive account in *Edward Thomas: a Portrait*, they present a refreshingly human picture of the poet which, as he himself wrote of Keats, shows 'he thought as much about women as most young men with a strong vein of sensuality and sensuousness'. To some extent starved of affection within his own family (the poem 'I may come near to loving you' about his father was too painful to be printed until long after the latter's death), Thomas found in Helen an anchor against the turbulence of his inner life and the disappointments of his literary career. He was, as he admitted himself, a difficult person to live with, and Helen tells us in *As It Was* that before marriage she recognised 'only now and then' what she called 'hints of this darkness in his soul'. There were times when both feared they were bad for each other, but it is difficult not to conclude that Edward would have had a still more unsettled life without her.

In March 1898, after a period as a non-collegiate student, he won a history scholarship to Lincoln College, Oxford. His first book, *The Woodland Life* (1897), in the main a collection of already published articles, appeared even before he became an undergraduate, and showed those faults of forced rhetoric he later so bitterly criticised:

> Wreathed in amongst the lower oak-sprays a bine of honeysuckle yet bears one crown of fragrant blossom. This single flower calls up memories of June, with its wild roses, the song of Philomel, and its long happy days rung in and out by the wild music of the blackcap: there is summer in its faint perfume.

Style and ideas here come from the common literary stock in the possession of such eminent second-raters as Alfred Austin, whose 'Garden' books, with their sunny view of South England nature, had gained a vogue in the nineties. When Thomas, in the same work, shuns artifice, the results are immediate and come close to the vividness of Hopkins's visualised detail in the *Journals*: 'Caterpillar abroad on a grass-blade – beautiful with orange, black, dun, and blue in stripes and spots'.

It was in June 1899 that Helen, now pregnant, married Edward in the Fulham Registry Office, an event greeted with a very mixed reception from both sets of parents, and particularly distasteful to Helen's mother. Among his unconventional qualities as a son-in-law, Edward had no religious affiliations: to the end of his life he was uninterested in and hostile to this aspect of human experience. His father, a Unitarian, later a Positivist (or humanist), had imposed some form of religious observance on his family, and looking back to his childhood Edward recalled Sunday observance as 'cruel and ceremonious punishments for the freedom of Monday to Saturday'. In place of this 'dead language' he and Helen shared a simple naturalism, and his poetry was to have no religious dimension in the normal sense of the word.

At Oxford, where he continued his journalism, he was able to live a more extrovert life, but when he finished in June 1900 with only a second in history, and still determined on writing as a career, his father's disillusion was complete. His mother, however, took care of Helen at Clapham during the first impoverished year of marriage, while a small legacy together with some literary earnings enabled Edward to begin looking after the now growing family: Merfyn, the first of three children, was born in January 1900.

Geographically, as well as emotionally, restlessness was to be the keynote of the remaining 17 years of Thomas's life. There were nine changes of house, all rented and all in country areas of Hampshire, Kent and Essex, as well as vacations and working holidays spent in Wales, Lancashire, East Anglia and elsewhere, culminating in the various moves of his army life. Significantly, his poetry is full of travel associations in the form of walking, roads, lanes, paths, railways and inns, methods and occasions of escape. But paradoxically travel is also a seeking for something – a place of rest, an answer to restlessness,

> At hawthorn-time in Wiltshire travelling
> In search of something chance would never bring.

It is a search for an idealisation of 'home', for permanence and peace, a yearning for the eternal which in the end lies at the root of restlessness.

After a brief and miserable stay in London, the family moved in September 1901 to Rose Acre Cottage at Bearsted, near Maidstone, an ugly house in beautiful surroundings, of which he wrote in *The Icknield Way* that it never came to feel like home: 'To this day it remains a body, and dead'. The Thomases never left the country for any substantial period after this: it fulfilled that paradoxical function which he described in *The Country* when he wrote that we go there 'to escape ourselves', but eventually 'we truly find ourselves'.

In 1902 he began what was to be a much valued connection as a reviewer with the *Daily Chronicle*, but the struggle against financial insolvency rarely slackened. If the Thomases were never 'poor', his efforts to keep up producing the necessary articles (and later books) had to be unremitting. He complained in despair in October 1902, 'I have to live by reviewing,' and in June 1905, 'The result of all my reviewing seems to be that I lose all power except of saying what a thing is not . . . . Original writing I dream about, but never get so far as to get out paper and pen for it'. As to giving up being an author and taking a humdrum job, the prospect was almost too awful to contemplate: like George Borrow, he believed

'Once an author, ever an author', even though the emotional strain was heavy. 'The only thing to be said for [reviewing] is that it produces money, which produces food and clothing for aged parents, fair wives, innocent children'. One of his first biographers gives a list of a typical week's reading, which ranged from 'Tchaikowsky's *Life and Letters*' through a further eleven titles to 'A Frenchman on Charles Lamb'. The effect of this type of work can be compared with the despair of Gerard Manley Hopkins – also worsened by frustrated creativity – over the immense number of exam papers he had to mark as classics professor in Dublin. The pressures contributed to fears of madness in both men.

This dark side of Thomas vies in his poetry with moments of high exhilaration, indeed is perhaps an inevitable complement to them. A preoccupation with death, and even thoughts of suicide appear in both his public and private writing, in his essays and tales, and in poems like 'Rain', which echoes the death-wish of a similar passage in *The Icknield Way*. Yet the man whose introspectiveness reached such depths was also an attractive and sociable companion who won the affection of many good friends, particularly where some shared literary interest was involved. From 1905–6 he looked after the crippled poet W. H. Davies; Robert Frost came to feel for him as a brother; Walter de la Mare had warm personal feelings for him and has a memorable description of the expression on Edward Thomas's face when they first met in a London café, 'whimsical, stealthy, shy, ardent, mocking, ironical, by turns', words which are almost equally appropriate to Thomas's poetry.

In December 1906 the Thomases moved to Berryfield Cottage at Steep, near Petersfield, in Hampshire:

This house and the country about it make the most beautiful place we ever lived in. We are now become people of whom passers by stop to think: How fortunate are they within those walls. I know it. I have thought the same as I came to the house and forgot it was my own.

The ironic tone only hints at the tragic feelings beneath, now perhaps perilously close to the surface: 'I sat thinking about ways of killing myself . . . I hate my work, my reviewing; my best I feel is negligible: I have no vitality, no originality, no love. I do harm'. Yet the same period produced two of his best prose works, *The South Country* and *Richard Jefferies* (1909), in the fields of travel-writing and critical biography respectively. Thomas, however, was no topographer: he cultivated a highly developed impressionism, so that his travels are more important as a reflection of his personality than as an account of a particular region.

Most of his travelling was in the South of England (though the picture of Haweswater in the Lake District in an essay called 'Midsummer' is one of his finest) and his writing has characteristic anticipations of his poetry. Thus, in *The South Country*, in advance of a poem like 'The Glory', he tells us that when the traveller has enumerated all that forms a country scene, 'much remains over, imponderable but mighty. Often when the lark is high he seems to be singing in some keyless chamber of the brain'. Such a transcendental sense of nature is often suggested in Jefferies, and since Thomas had stayed in Swindon in his boyhood and grown to love Jefferies's work, to write his life was a labour of love. It is a biography in the nineteenth-century style, quoting a good deal of Jefferies's own writing; critical discussion is limited, but always sympathetic, and the personality of the subject remains Thomas's chief interest.

Thomas sent his children to Bedales, the progressive school in Steep village, where Helen also taught, although he had no interest himself in educational theory, or indeed in political or social ideas in the abstract. Even his private letters show a marked lack of comment on 'questions of the day'. He did attempt to take on the responsibility of a job by working for the Royal Commission of Ancient Monuments in the latter part of 1908, but the regular desk work it involved was anathema to him, and it was abandoned in six months.

The Thomases were offered a new house to rent, later called Wick Green, on Ashford Hanger, a mile or so above Steep village; the builder, Geoffrey Lupton, was a follower of William Morris, and the house was decorated accordingly. It was occupied before the end of 1909, and from its magnificent situation some 400 feet up above Steep Valley, there were long views across the rolling countryside to the South Downs. There was a study separate from the main house which Edward was able to go on using even when (inevitably) another move came, down into Steep village itself.

Yet it was not a happy house: the poems 'The New House' and 'Wind and Mist' describe his gloomy sensations in what turned out to be a bleak and windswept situation, and in September 1911 he went through one of his worst spells of depression, in which his future seemed less certain than ever before. 'Things get so rapidly worse,' he wrote, 'that something must happen soon inside my head or outside'; and again, 'I have somehow lost my balance and can never recover it by diet or rule or any deliberate means, but only by some miracle from within or without. If I don't recover it and causes of worry continue I must go smash.' During this period he wrote some of his least inspired work, *Feminine Influence on the Poets*, *Maurice Maeterlinck* and *The Icknield Way*, and matters were made worse by his fear that he would drag down with him Helen and the three young children of whom he was now the father.

Things improved in 1912 when he started to receive treatment from a sympathetic and personable young doctor, Godwin Baynes, and at the same time, in his studies of Walter Pater (1913) and other writers, he began consciously to reject those rhetorical conventions he had once admired. He wrote to his poet–and dramatist–friend Gordon Bottomley in March 1912: 'I am only just learning how ill my notes have been making me write by all but destroying such natural rhythms as I have in me. Criticising Pater has helped the discovery'. Further attacks on ornate prose style came in his books on Swinburne and Lafcadio Hearn, where his remarks reflect an imagination in process of freeing itself, as if in readiness for the poems he was to write two years later. The critical studies themselves are not important as criticism, and Thomas had no gift for the historical approach (as Sir John Squire was later to point out in the *New Statesman*); it is in his reviews, of which a fine sample is printed in Edna Longley's *A Language Not to be Betrayed*, that his wide sympathies and literary sensitivity are seen to best advantage, entitling him to an individual place in twentieth-century criticism.

In summer 1913 came the move to Yew Tree Cottage in the village of Steep itself, and a few months later his first meeting with Robert Frost, who was to have so crucial an influence on the remainder of Thomas's career. Frost was thirty-nine, a published poet in both the USA and England, though in neither country possessing the reputation for which he longed. Like Thomas, he felt unfulfilled in his present way of life, and like him had contemplated suicide. In literature, he was already pursuing the goal which Thomas was more slowly becoming aware of, the need for naturalness in rhythm and language, as well as, in Frost's particular case, the use of incidents from ordinary life in poetry.

It was not, however, until the following summer, the fateful one of 1914, that the two got to know each other well, when Edward and Helen holidayed with the Frosts in the lovely countryside of the Herefordshire–Gloucestershire border. To the Frosts, Edward was 'quite the most admirable and lovable man we have ever known', while in Helen's later recollection, 'It was at once obvious that Robert and Edward were very congenial to each other'. Their long discussions about literature and their reading of each other's work led to Frost's certainty that Edward's vocation was poetry, a conclusion that another friend of Thomas's, the writer W. H. Hudson, had come to after reading *The Happy-Go-Lucky Morgans*, Thomas's autobiographical novel: 'He is essentially a poet . . . You noticed probably in reading the book that every person described in it . . . [is] one and all just Edward Thomas. A poet trying to write prose fiction often does this'. For his own part, Frost had observed that many passages in Thomas's travel-writing, in their train of thought and choice and handling of language and imagery, were already close to poetry. In fact, when Thomas came to write verse, he re-used, not necessarily consciously, some of this earlier material.

The outbreak of war led to Frost's return to America early in 1915, accompanied by Merfyn, with the possibility that Thomas would follow and try his luck with teaching and writing in the USA. But Edward was beginning to reflect on his own possible role in the European conflict, and his suggestion to his literary agent of a series of essays about the 'war's influence' on life in different parts of England resulted in a number of outstanding pieces published in 1914–15, which may be read in the posthumous collection *The Last Sheaf*. He also prepared *This England*, an anthology of poems and prose extracts which gave a wide interpretation to the idea of patriotism, avoiding 'professedly patriotic writing' for 'indirect praise'. The possibility of showing his love for England in a more concrete way was also in his mind, but far from militaristic, his mood was that of a latter-day Coleridge, as he described him in his *Literary Pilgrim in England*, 'a tolerably complete Englishman, aware of the follies both of peace and war'.

This mature attitude was another source of disagreement between himself and his jingoistic father.

Having told Eleanor Farjeon in October 1913 that he 'couldn't write a poem to save his life', some time late in 1914 verse began to come to him and to continue to do so with remarkable regularity over the next two years. No one reason can be offered for the emergence of poetry at this point in his life: the two most obvious, Frost and the war, seem too obvious, although no doubt they played their part. Frost wrote retrospectively that 'Edward Thomas had about lost patience with the minor poetry it was his business to review . . . Right at that moment [1914] he was writing as good poetry as anybody alive, but in prose form from where it did not declare itself'. The modern novelist and critic, John Wain, suggests that until that moment (for whatever reason) 'self-consciousness' had been the factor that had prevented an earlier breakthrough, and Paul Cubieta, writing in the *New England Quarterly*, in July 1979, blames Thomas – somewhat unfairly in view of his family responsibilities – for lacking the 'artistic courage' to make the change sooner from his career of journeyman writer.

By March 1915 he was revelling, if a little uncertainly, in the new freedom: 'You cannot imagine how eagerly I have run up this by-way and how anxious I am to be sure it is not a cul-de-sac'. For the time being, editors would not accept his poems: he wrote wryly of one rejection: 'I suppose Blackwood just thought it looked very much like prose and was puzzled by the fact that it was got up like verse'. They were all submitted, through Eleanor Farjeon, under the pseudonym of Edward Eastaway, and it may have been their continued rejection, as well as patriotic reasons, that led him in July 1915 to enlist in the Artists' Rifles, and resist for the time being Frost's invitation to the States. 'His entrance into military life . . . suggests . . . an action to test the purpose life might have for him' (W. A. Sutton, *Southern Review* (Louisiana), July 1975, p. 692). It was a way of finding out about himself, just as his poetry became a process of self-exploration; like Alun Lewis, the Second World War poet, he too could have written that there was 'a worse battle than war or peace to fight – the heart is my battleground, a bloody place'.

Military training began in August, and there was a temporary pause in the writing of poetry, but in the anthology *This England*, which appeared in October, he included two poems by himself,

'The Manor Farm' and 'Haymaking', under the usual pseudonym (the first two of his poems ever to appear in print had come out earlier that year in an obscure 'art' periodical called *Root and Branch*). Both poems are a characteristically indirect expression of his patriotism, in line with the purpose explained in the preliminary 'Note' that the editor was:

> excluding professedly patriotic writing because it is generally bad and because indirect praise is sweeter and more profound, – never aiming at what a committee from Great Britain and Ireland might call complete, – I wished to make a book as full of English character and country as an egg is of meat.

'Do you know what you are fighting for?' Eleanor Farjeon asked him (*Edward Thomas: the Last Four Years*, p. 154). 'He stopped, and picked up a pinch of earth. "Literally, for this." He crumbled it between finger and thumb, and let it fall.'

He was now a lance-corporal and an instructor with particular responsibility for map-reading at Hare Hall Camp, near Romford in Essex. In June 1916 he applied for a commission in the Royal Garrison Artillery, which was duly granted. All accounts suggest he was a good soldier: conscientious, kindly and, despite being older than most with whom he mixed, fitting in well with his comrades. He may have been a Hamlet, as Eleanor Farjeon suggested – and as another introspective soldier–poet and contemporary, Ivor Gurney described himself – but, like Hamlet, he was popular with many around him. Although he found many aspects of the military life boring and suffered from homesickness, the more morbid aspects of his depression were now thrown off. His experience was bearing out in a remarkable way a prophecy he had made many years before the war began: 'Only a revolution or a catastrophe or an improbable development can ever make calm or happiness possible for me'.

His application for a commission meant more training in the Royal Artillery. He intended going to France as soon as possible, although he had every opportunity of remaining in England as an instructor if he wished: 'I am rather impatient to go out and be shot at. That is all I want, to do something if I am discovered to be of any use, but in any case to be made to run risks, to be put through it'. War was a personal test, death a challenge rather than deterrent; Alun Lewis, too, chose action, and possible death, instead of home duties.

More training in London (September 1916) was followed by camp at Trowbridge in Wiltshire, the country of his favourite writer, Richard Jefferies. In November his book on Keats appeared. Keats's devotion to a life of literature, his love of the senses, as well as, paradoxically, a fascination with death, all found a response in Thomas, whose progress towards that final test came a stage nearer the same month when he received his commission as 2nd Lieutenant in the Royal Garrison Artillery. He was posted to 244 Siege Battery and expected to go soon to France.

During this last year he had plenty of opportunity to spend weekends and short holidays with Helen and the family, as well as with other friends. He had lost his study at Wick Green and Helen had fallen out with the Bedales staff, and they now lived at High Beech in Epping Forest, where Edward spent the Christmas of 1916. There was a final leave early in 1917 (the last farewell is movingly described by Helen in *World Without End*), and at the end of January he and his battery, of which he was the oldest member, sailed to Le Havre.

The diary which he had now begun to keep shows him as accepting the conditions of army life without losing his sensitivity to the world around him, especially its natural beauty. Two days before he left England for France, it was 'a clear windy frosty dawn, the sun like a bright coin between the knuckles of opposite hills seen from sidelong'. In very cold weather they crossed northern France to their emplacement at Arras, where preparations were in hand for the Allies' Easter offensive. Thomas spent his time observing the enemy or engaged in the heterogeneous tasks of a junior officer, and was stoically content:

There are so many things to enjoy [he wrote in his last letter to Frost], and if I remember rightly not more to regret than say a year or ten years ago. I think I get surer of some primitive things that one has got to be sure of, about oneself and other people . . . In short, I am glad I came out and I think less about return than I thought I should. (R. G. Thomas, *Edward Thomas, a Portrait*, p. 286.)

On 13 March 1917, *An Annual of New Poetry*, edited by his friend and fellow-poet Gordon Bottomley, published eighteen poems by 'Edward Eastaway', and in the *Times Literary Supplement* he was able to read and be irritated by what was, in fact, a generally sympathetic review, its main complaint being that his senses were stronger than his spiritual vision. A few days after he had read this review, on Easter Monday, 9 April, at 7.30 in the morning, he was killed by the blast of a shell while on duty. He was buried at nearby Agny. His commanding officer wrote of him: 'His serene and kindly presence and quiet, dry humour did much to alleviate the squalid miseries of life for his companions'. Shortly after the news, his father revealed the identity of 'Eastaway' in *The Times*. In October, his *Poems* was published.

Coincidentally, Ivor Gurney, himself a neglected poet, (who was later to set some of Thomas's poems to music), was wounded on Good Friday. A day or so before Gurney had written: 'This morning was beautifully sunny, and daisies are poking their heads out here and there – without steel helmets! O the Spring, the Spring! Come late or early, you must give hope ever to the dwellers in the house of flesh'. Thomas's poetry flowered late, and his full reputation still later, but the poems have brought increasing joy and inspiration to 'fellow-dwellers' of the flesh. His personality was still being commemorated in volumes of reminiscence twenty years later, but it is in the poems, elusive and ambiguous, that we best find, most powerfully find, what Thomas is.

3 THOMAS AND THE LITERARY BACKGROUND

The writer to whom Thomas owed most in spirit was Richard Jefferies (1848–1887), journalist and country-writer, pagan and mystic. Thomas had known his work from his boyhood when he had taken as his motto the concluding words of one of Jefferies's most famous books, *The Amateur Poacher*: 'Let us get out of these indoor narrow modern days, whose twelve hours somehow have become shortened, into the sunlight and the pure wind. A something that the ancients called divine can be found and felt there still'. In a series of nature books that culminated spiritually in *The Story of My Heart* (1883), Jefferies revealed a deep knowledge of country life and a mystic, semi-religious sense of Nature, which only a tragically early death, like Thomas's, prevented from achieving final, mature expression.

In details and certain general ideas, the reader of Thomas will recognise many clues and parallels in Jefferies's writing. The character of Lob, the archetypal Englishman, is anticipated in a variety of contexts: for example, in the essay 'Field Words and Ways' when Jefferies writes that 'The labouring people seem in all their ways and speech to be different, survivals perhaps of a time when their words and superstitions were the ways of a ruder England'; in the charcoal-burner of 'The Countryside: Sussex'; and in the Hodge of *The Nature Diaries and Note-Books*, of whom Jefferies declares: 'In truth Hodge has been the mainstay of England these 1,000 years, battle and breeze, but has had no voice.' Starting-points for other poems by Thomas are suggested by such essays as 'Hours of Spring', which opens with an account of the evocative beauty of bird-song, and 'Winds of Heaven' (all in the posthumous collection *Field and Hedgerow*, 1889), which attempts to capture the mysterious sound of wind blowing around a house.

But, above all, Jefferies responds to the mystery of Nature and its seeming indifference to human attempts to comprehend it. Like Thomas in 'The Glory', Jefferies too, when he described the 'beauty of the morning', wished for 'some increase or enlargement of his existence to correspond with the largeness of feeling' (*The Story of My Heart*). Elsewhere he wished for 'wider feelings, more extended sympathies', and described an experience common to Thomas when he concluded that 'appreciation of beauty is often a deep sense of our own unworthiness and lack'. In comparing these two writers, the modern poet and critic P. J. Kavanagh suggested in *The Listener*, 15 June 1978, that the quality of 'ecstasy and self-surrender' in Jefferies's *Story of My Heart* was impossible for Thomas. Joy, in fact, does exist in Thomas's poetry, for example in 'Adlestrop' and 'The Brook', but there is restraint in its expression, as if the author feared for its fragility.

Thomas was well read in the Romantic poets, and both William Wordsworth and John Keats, though for different reasons, are important in understanding his place in the English literary tradition. Wordsworth's dependence on Nature is more profound than Thomas's because it is not merely personal, but leads to a philosophy which encompasses the whole of mankind. While its religious element is foreign to the outlook of Thomas, who followed Jefferies in believing, 'Nothing good to man but man', such transcendental experiences as the young Wordsworth on Windermere standing and watching 'Till all was tranquil as a dreamless sleep' must have been immediately understood by the author of 'Ambition' and 'The Brook'. Moreover, Wordsworth's revolutionary views on language in 1798, although not fully carried out in practice, bear comparison with Thomas's criticism of rhetoric and praise of speech rhythms in verse: it is clear that for both, language had a crucial role in any new departure in poetry.

Thomas was drawn to Keats, both as man and poet. There are many traces of Keatsian diction in his verse–often to its disadvantage–as well as more specific echoes, but it is the sense of yearning and dissatisfaction with life found in the Odes that offers a more important parallel. Here is the melancholy and sometimes love for death that will remind readers of Thomas of 'Rain' or 'Melancholy', and which the critic Hugh Underhill identifies when he writes that both poets were concerned with the problems of escape from, yet reconciliation with, life. Thomas's reading of Keats confirmed one of his favourite notions about the inseparability of pleasure and pain in human experience; as he wrote in his book on Keats, the 'Ode to Melancholy' 'seems to say that the bitter with the sweet is worthwhile – is the necessary woof of life'.

Thomas has often been associated with the rural tradition, a somewhat vague phrase applied to that interest in country things which English writers have shown over many centuries. The conventions of this form of writing are many and various, its exponents wide-ranging. Thomas's most famous immediate predecessor was Jefferies, while among his contemporaries were W. H. Hudson, whose books reflected a life spent partly in South America, partly in Southern England, and Thomas Hardy, whose settings, themes and language, in novel and verse, show his knowledge of and feeling for Wessex man. For Hardy and Thomas, the natural world is not simply background, but is used to modify and express the mood of the poet. The implications are admittedly different: Thomas looks inward to his own self, his poetry throwing light on his own quizzical, sometimes inspired, sometimes tortured character; Hardy's poetry offers a sort of 'philosophy' of life, ironic, stoic, and virtually consistent from poem to poem.

In his essay 'The Hardy Tradition in Modern English Poetry', Professor Hynes has included Thomas among those poets who share with Hardy a 'religious' view of man, that is, that 'man and nature participate in a common natural order'; in this sense a religious poem deals 'on however small a scale, with man's relations with the universe'. It can easily be seen how poems like 'Birds' Nests', 'Adlestrop', 'The Path', 'Tall Nettles', and many others fulfil the further definition that

In such poems the subject is ordinary physical reality; but that reality includes a sense of immanence, or aura, of the presence of permanence and value in the humblest particulars of the earth. (Hynes, 'The Hardy Tradition in Modern English Poetry', reprinted in *The Thomas Hardy Journal*, October 1986, p. 37.)

There are also interesting parallels in form between the two poets. Although the quantity and variety of Thomas's verse forms cannot compare with Hardy's, both, nevertheless, experiment with some freedom in the search for appropriate expression. Both use the diction and rhythms of common speech, as well as deliberately awkward and 'poetic' language and syntax for planned effect: compare, for example, Hardy's selection of grotesque diction in the 'Convergence of the Twain' to emphasise that very quality in the conception of the poem, with Thomas's transition to the elevated language that brings 'The Manor Farm' to its desired climax. Finally, a comparison can be drawn between what C. H. Sisson calls Hardy's 'lack of pretension' and the unpretentiousness of Thomas's own poetry, with its absence of rhetorical flourish and grand declaration, and preference for the quieter truths of understatement.

'Georgian' poetry was also interested in the countryside, and Thomas has often been associated with the Georgian poets whose period of greatest influence was in the second decade of the twentieth century. When Edward Marsh produced the first of the five volumes of *Georgian Poetry* in 1912, he believed, with Rupert Brooke who helped to suggest the title, that English poetry was 'once again putting on a new strength and beauty'. When the last volume appeared in 1922, he had demonstrated that there was a market for poetry provided the more progressive and controversial names were avoided. This meant no Eliot, nor any poem which seriously challenged traditional views of intelligibility and form, with the result that 'Georgian' eventually became a dismissive label for the naive and the conventional. Thomas reviewed the first volume:

It shows much beauty, strength, and mystery, and some magic – much aspiration, less defiance, no revolt–and it brings out with great cleverness many sides of the modern love of the simple and primitive, as seen in children, peasants, savages, early men, animals, and Nature in general.

The element of gentle mockery here suggests it was not Thomas's ideal of poetry, despite those later writers and editors who have identified him with the group. An attempt to include him in one of the later Georgian volumes published after his death was thwarted by Marsh on the grounds that only living poets were eligible. Thomas's poetry would not have seemed, at least at first sight, greatly out of place, but compared with much by other Georgian poets that appeared, his work is more original, more tightly argued, and more responsive to the sensitivity of language.

Language, especially in its expression as speech, is the key to the relationship between Frost and Thomas as poets. Both believed that the language of verse should possess some of the qualities of normal speech, avoiding rhetoric and seeking to imitate the rhythms of the speaking voice. Frost wrote to a correspondent in February 1914, at the beginning of his friendship with Thomas:

> To judge a poem or piece of prose you go the same way to work – apply the one test – greatest test. You listen for the sentence sounds. If you find some of those not bookish, caught fresh from the mouths of people . . . you know you have found a writer.

The emphasis here is on the adoption of speech rhythms, but in practice, as may be seen in *North of Boston*, this inevitably implied a rejection of 'poetic diction'. When Thomas reviewed Frost, he could announce with pleasure that

> These poems are revolutionary because they lack the suggestion of rhetoric, and even at first sight appear to lack that poetic intensity of which rhetoric is an imitation. Their language is free from poetical words and forms that are the chief material of secondary poets.

A characteristic of Thomas's diction is the mixture of nineteenth-century poetic language with that of contemporary (educated) speech, contributing to that deliberate awkwardness which one critic, Geoffrey Thurley (*The Ironic Harvest*, London, 1974, p. 33) considers a virtue by comparison with the glib quality which he finds in Frost's verse. Thomas's catholicity is in line with the advice of fellow-poet Lascelles Abercrombie (see p. 74) also writing in February 1914, who pleaded for the spoken word as the basis of poetic expression, though not to the exclusion from consideration of the total stock of the English language.

Thomas's place in the tradition of 'modern' poetry is as debatable as the concept of modern poetry itself. There is no obvious way in which he fits into what Thurley calls the 'intellectualist', post-Metaphysical tendency, seen in Eliot, Pound, and Empson: he is neither scholarly, allusive, nor detached. On the other hand, his influence has been seen in Larkin and Hughes, while Isherwood claimed he was one of the models of the early Auden. Like Professor Hynes, Andrew Motion places him in what he calls the 'evolutionary', rather than revolutionary tradition of twentieth-century English verse, including Larkin, Hughes, and R.S. Thomas in the line of descent: understatement, economy of style, and a humanist outlook are attributes they share. However Edward Thomas is finally classified, his contribution to twentieth-century poetry seems assured of the critical respect due to one who honestly strove to be himself as much in literature as in life.

4 COMMENTARY

Except where additional poems have been introduced – see prefatory note – the order followed is that of the Faber and Faber selection, edited by R. S. Thomas, which is not chronological. Professor R. G. Thomas thinks that read in order of composition the poems 'reveal a consistent development', yet some of the best ('Old Man' and 'The Manor Farm') were among the earliest written. The correct order of dating is probably of more concern to the biographer than to the student and critic. R. S. Thomas's arrangement is in any case interesting for its own sake: in 'And You, Helen' we recognise the poet's wry regret at failure to know himself, before passing on to 'The Other', in which such ignorance becomes a matter of tragic self-analysis. The grand celebration of Englishness, 'Lob', contrasts with the unassuming 'Tall Nettles', whose ordinariness is another insight into the poet's love of the English scene. Students of Edward Thomas can continue to examine for themselves the parallels and contrasts in successive poems.

'The Unknown Bird'

The poem was written in January 1915, and the lines in which Thomas refers to his state of mind 'Four years, or five' before, 'sometimes suffering/A heavy body and a heavy heart' might be recalling the period of intense depression he went through in 1911.

The poem is a celebration of both memory and mystery, two themes often found in Georgian verse. Thomas begins by recollecting the song of a bird in a wood several years ago: it stirred him profoundly, but no one could tell him what bird it was. He still recalls the song clearly as a mixture of joy and sadness, but however happy or unhappy his life really was when he first heard the bird, now, when he thinks back to that time he experiences a sense of exhilaration. (Lines 23–6, in a typical paradox, acknowledge that sadness contains joy, but he can no longer feel the sadness.)

The poem hints that the experience may have been an illusion: he was by himself, no one else heard it, nor recognises the song which he describes, but by bringing a sense of happiness, whether based on illusion or not, the experience justifies itself. (There is also an unseen cuckoo in the essay 'Midsummer' which is printed in *The Last Sheaf*.) Jan Marsh, in *Edward Thomas, a Poet for his Country*, suggests that the bird 'stands as a symbol of the elusive joy Thomas could never quite capture in the present moment'.

The idea of memory transmuting experience appears elsewhere in Thomas: in the last lines of 'October', and in *The South Country*, p. 133: 'I recall many scenes . . . I do not recall happiness in them, yet the moment I return to them in fancy I am happy'. Memory is also important in Wordsworth's poetry, where the dancing daffodils lighten the suffering of later life, and the Highland girl's song will probably have the same after-effect. In 'Tintern Abbey' Wordsworth recognises the consolation brought by memories of visiting the Wye. The influence of Keats's 'Ode to a Nightingale', with the nightingale's power to liberate the imagination, must also be recognised here.

In its form the poem is distinctively Thomas's: a blank verse monologue in which the sentence overrides the line-structure without destroying the powerful position of the last word in the line. Even 'Then' (line 20) makes a strong line-ending in a poem which takes the reader through past, present and future. There is a notable feeling for speech-rhythms, although diction and syntax vary between the poetic and the informal: compare

> but others never sang
> In that great beech-wood all that May and June.
> No one saw him.

with

> Yet that he travelled through the trees and sometimes
> Neared me, was plain, though somehow distant still
> He sounded.

The contrast is not excessive, but enough to underline the distinction in the poem between the reality of the narrator and the elusiveness of the experience he is trying to recapture. The poem avoids the Georgian pitfall of mere nostalgia by the stubbornness with which Thomas pursues his argument, even at the risk of almost exasperating over-subtlety:

> Sad more than joyful it was, if I must say
> That it was one or other, but if sad
> 'Twas sad only with joy too, too far off
> For me to taste it.

It is the 'joy' which is too far off, but the awkwardness of these lines might well suggest the poet has sacrificed clarity for honesty in trying to convey the nuances of the experience.

'But These Things Also'

From the mystery of 'The Unknown Bird', we turn to the down-to-earth detail recorded by Thomas's observant eye as he remarks the changing of the seasons. It is not beauty, but 'inscape' that appeals to him, Hopkins's name for the experience of any distinctive and individual feature of phenomena, however mean. Verse two is a succession of such inscapes. This is not a traditional poem about Spring, as is suggested by the defiant opening lines rejecting the usual poetic clichés for the season. The form, too, refuses to be conventional: one long sentence, marked by almost constant enjambment – unpunctuated movement from the end of one line to the next – studiously avoids climaxes and rhetorical emphasis, as the narrator ruminates, rather than takes any more assertive stance.

'Tears'

At first sight the two scenes have no connection, but both in their own way celebrate Englishness (the soldiers, significantly, are 'countrymen') and both are associated, actually or potentially, with violence and death. The poem was written in January 1915 when Thomas was reflecting on the nature of his own responsibilities in the war. He makes no statement here, his aim being rather to convey a feeling of great intensity, and he may be remembering a parallel to the Tower incident which occurs in Jefferies's *The Story of My Heart* and which he quoted in his life of Jefferies:

> So subtle is the chord of life that sometimes to watch troops marching in rhythmic order, undulating along the column as the feet are lifted, brings tears in my eyes.

Tears as the expression of a profound, if inexplicable, emotion also occur in Thomas's story, 'The First of Spring': 'The weather which filled her with a desire to do more than she had ever done before, left her at the same time as weak as a child and on the edge of inexplicable tears'. A similar experience of unbidden tears is described in his biography of George Borrow: 'Was it the beauty of the scene which gave rise to these emotions?'

Of the first two lines, a contemporary reviewer wrote that Thomas

> uses none of the loose phrases into which many a lesser but more widely acknowledged poet would have been betrayed. He does not say 'There are no tears for crying' or 'Weeping is done, tears' chains are rusted o'er'. He says he has no tears left, and then writes a line in the grand manner, which in him alone of twentieth-century poets seems to live on only a little lessened, 'Their ghosts, if tears have ghosts, did fall' (*London Mercury*, January 1927)

'Blooming Meadow' was a real place, near Elses Farm in Kent, where the Thomases lived 1904–6. Helen speaks of its 'lovely slope' in *World Without End*.

'The Lane'

Lanes, and other dark and secret places, are common in Thomas. Helen describes such a lane leading to their house at Wick Green: 'The winding lane which led to the outer world was the darkest lane I have ever known; so deep and dark it was that the entrance to it on the main road looked like the entrance to a tunnel'. Such a description, however, is more appropriate to the lane of 'Women He Liked' than the present poem with its atmosphere of peace and beauty and names from the Steep area. The four seasons are mingled in a characteristic Thomas fashion, and the lane provides an idyllic refuge from the world of real time. The conclusion is as satisfying as, though different in intensity from, 'Old Man', with its repetition of 'same', crucial positioning of 'until', and the speaking voice's stress on 'is'. It is not entirely clear what Thomas meant by 'waters that no vessel ever sailed', and the dots at the end of line 8 may indicate that the poem was written in two stages (as R. G. Thomas suggests).

'The Combe'

In *The South Country* Thomas describes a combe as one of those 'steep-sided bays, running and narrowing far into and up the sides of the chalk hills . . . [Their] steep sides are clothed with beeches, thousands of beeches'. But the poem is no piece of cheerful nature painting: the death of the badger may be seen from one point of view as representing the destruction of a traditional part of the English scene, and from another it may carry associations with the war in France (the poem was written in December 1914). The ancientness of the Combe is intensified in a sinister way by the killing, and whereas the dark of the first line is something natural to the Combe's age and location, in line 9 it has come to carry a sense of evil.

Like 'The Path' this poem avoids the use of a narrator, distancing the reader, and leaving him to draw his own conclusions about any profounder meaning. Like an abbreviated sonnet, the last three and a half lines are the twist in the argument, where the poet launches the final stage in what he has to say. Before this, the jerky movement of lines 2–6 and their abrupt syllables suggest the rough terrain:

Its mouth is stopped with bramble, thorn, and briar;
And no one scrambles over the sliding chalk
By beech and yew and perishing juniper
Down the half precipices of its sides, with roots
And rabbit holes for steps.

The last three and a half lines swell out to an emphatic conclusion
as Thomas implies his protest at the badger's death.

'And You, Helen'

This is the last in a group of four poems, written March–April
1916, which Thomas himself described as 'household poems'.
Each one relates the gift he would wish to give to the different
members of his family, but of all of them this is the most revealing.
In his *Feminine Influence on the Poets* (1910) Thomas had noted
that women suffered from the male character of society, and here
he regrets his own part in depriving Helen of her personality. The
poem is a confession and touches on many aspects of their married
life, as well as reminding us that, whereas Edward had good
eyesight, Helen was short-sighted (and often wore glasses). It
culminates, typically, not in some banal statement about their life
together, but in Thomas's admission that he does not know the
nature of his own personality; in the next poem he attempts to
explore this mystery. The octosyllabic is his favourite line: the
couplets he uses here are appropriate to the familiar and sometimes lighthearted tone he adopts, although this conceals deeper
misgivings.

'The Other'

Curiously perhaps for so elaborate a poem on the other self – and
proof maybe of the immediate psychological relief poetry provided
him – this was one of Thomas's earliest poems (probably written
December 1914). The true subject is not his schizophrenia, but the
profound sense of rootlessness and inferiority which frequently
made him feel the pointlessness of his own life; awareness of
another self perhaps springs from loss of confidence in one's ability

to deal with life. Thomas wrote: 'A sort of conspiracy is going on [in my head] which leaves me only a joint tenancy and a perpetual scare of the other tenant and wonder what he will do'. In his prose work, *In Pursuit of Spring*, completed shortly before he began writing poetry, he describes a figure called the 'Other Man' who shadows the author and represents, with some exaggeration, characteristics of the real Thomas. The theme of the double has always been popular in literature, and usually to sinister effect, as in Stevenson's *Dr Jekyll and Mr Hyde* ('My Hyde is worse', wrote Hopkins, acknowledging the book's psychological truth) and Edgar Allan Poe's *William Wilson*.

The form, eleven verses of ten octosyllabic lines – eight syllables and four heavy stresses each line – with only three rhymes in each verse, is as unusual as the subject-matter. Enjambment is used with extraordinary fluency, but there are several passages that are difficult to understand, in part because of the demands of the form:

Lines 29–30.   An inhospitable coast would be as unfriendly as the people the poet asked.

Lines 31–40.   He went on searching for this stranger, but only found satisfaction for less important aims and tasks. He wanted to satisfy profounder desires than this. He now begins to forget that he ever had any other purpose in life than this pursuit.

Lines 81–90.   A very difficult passage. I can only follow Longley's explanation. By the words 'happiness and powers . . . bowers' Thomas seems to be giving an alternative description of his state of mind. 'I' should be understood in front of 'smiled and enjoyed', and the sort of experience he described in the previous verse was a 'moment of everlastingness'. The last lines appear to state that in such experiences of melancholy he did not realise that finding out 'the Other' would be the solution he needed. Longley comments that the involved syntax illustrates the complex nature of the poet's thoughts, perhaps an over-charitable view of a failure to resolve them.

At the end of the poem, Thomas recognises that he will never be without his other self, and hence that dissatisfaction will always be his lot. Michael Kirkham, writing in *Ariel*, July 1975, sees 'The Other' as a poem in which Thomas accepts his social alienation and the probability that he would never achieve the integration which one side of him wanted.

'A Private'

One of the first of Thomas's poems to be printed (in *Six Poems*, 1916), the wartime reference is characteristically couched in the rural imagery with which he was most familiar. The poem is laconic – and ironic – in a way that would have appealed to Hardy, whose 'Drummer Hodge' also treats of a country lad who falls and is buried in an alien land. Both authors preserve a stoicism of emotion before the tragic fact, although the solemn tone adopted by Hardy leaves no place for the bitter 'joke' that Thomas creates out of the situation. The fate of Thomas's ploughman is as 'private' as his army rank, and his occasional peace-time habit of sleeping out-of-doors has now become permanent.

'March the Third'

This was the date of Thomas's birthday. The poem should be compared with the earlier 'March' in which Thomas also celebrates a day's birdsong, but with the suggestion that the thrushes have some secret knowledge which they share with the poet. 'March the Third' (through the voice of Helen Thomas) describes the beautiful blending of bells and birdsong on a Sunday, when each seems to take on some quality of the other: 'the birds' songs have the holiness gone from the bells'. The style typically lies somewhere between the colloquial and the 'poetic', but catches the tone of the speaking voice in many of the constructions:

> I think they blend
> Now better than they will when passed
> Is this unnamed, unmarked godsend

or

> but the birds' songs have
> the holiness gone from the bells.

'The Manor Farm'

This was the usual name originally given to the farm owned by the local land-owner and is still common in Southern England. There is one so called in the Steep area. The poem was actually written on Christmas Eve 1914, and first appeared in the following year in *This England*, the anthology selected by Thomas with the purpose of making a book 'as full of English character and country as an egg is of meat' (the poem's last line makes the connection). Instead of describing a conventional February day, Thomas writes of one in which all four seasons seem involved (compare 'The Lane'), preferring the evidence of his own personal observation and feelings. The details of the scene are powerfully evocative and escape any semblance of a 'dead' list of conventional imagery: each detail comes alive through the verb (and sometimes the adverb) with which it is associated: 'The rock-like mud unfroze', 'the catkins wagging', 'church and yew/ And farmhouse slept';

> Three cart-horses were looking over a gate
> Drowsily through their forelocks, swishing their tails
> Against a fly, a solitary fly.

The languorous inactivity of the last scene is suggested by the stressed position of 'drowsily' – its effect would be lost between 'were' and 'looking' – the onomatopoeic value of 'swishing' imitating the sound of the horses' tails, and the long caesura – or pause – that precedes the final phrase. Many other devices contribute to the atmosphere of the first section: the alliteration – repetition of same initial consonant – on 's', assonance (for example, the same vowel sound of 'down', 'sound', 'drowsily', lines 13–16), and the unforced balancing of short and longer sentences (or main clauses) against each other giving an air of ease and naturalness.

The success of the second section is more debatable. Rhetoric is consciously substituted for simplicity, the language of Keats for, as it were, Frost, and the implicit patriotic message of the main part has now become explicit.

The poem may have been influenced by a passage in an essay by Richard Jefferies, 'Out of Doors in February':

There is very often a warm interval in February . . . Released
from the grip of the frost, the streams trickle forth from the
fields . . . [The lark] gives us a few minutes of summer in
February days.

'The Gallows'

According to Thomas, this grim poem was inspired by stories that
he used to tell his second daughter, Myfanwy; perhaps the horrific
element was less prominent in the actual telling. The directness of
the writing, with its refrain and simple sentence construction, is
appropriate to a child's tale, but the lack of emotion with which the
deaths are recounted may reflect the shock to Thomas's own
feelings at the war news from France: the poem was written within
a few days of the opening of the battle of the Somme, 1 July 1916,
when 19,000 British soldiers were killed on the first day alone.
Each verse consists of a series of simply constructed clauses with a
refrain of two or three lines. The grimness is intensified by the
details of the lives of the now dead animals: the weasel 'lived in the
sun/With all his family'; the magpie could 'both talk and do – /But
what did that avail?' 'Many other beasts' were 'taken from their
feasts' and 'hung up' to swing and have endless leisure'.

All this horror may be seen as mirroring the indiscriminate
slaughter wrought by war, but at a deeper and more personal level
the poem seems inspired by a disgust for living itself. The refrain
'Without pleasure, without pain', as a description of death,
reduces life to a balancing act of the senses; 'no more sins to be
sinned' suggests life is an occasion of sin (and nothing more); 'to
swing and have endless leisure' is not necessarily an entirely ironic
assessment of the advantages of death – Thomas himself was
aware of the attraction of the (possibly) restful state of death.

'Out in the Dark'

This was the last but one poem written by Thomas (24 December
1916) before his departure for France, and was composed in his
last home, High Beech in the middle of Epping Forest, which
seems to have contributed to the deer, snow and general sense of
isolation. Darkness represents death, and the last verse is (ambi-
guously) suggesting that life only seems fragile to those who are

afraid of death. The heavy consonants of the rhyme in this last verse bring the poem to a powerful conclusion.

The poem's sinister atmosphere is reflected in its more technical aspects. The softness of the 's' and 'f' sounds in the first three verses contrast with the sharper 'l's and 't's of the last one, while assonance on the 'ah' sound – 'dark, fast, stars, & c' – also binds the first group of verses together. The short lines and frequent rhymes would normally seem more appropriate in a lighter poem, and here the effect is grotesque. The poem has often been compared with Thomas Hardy's 'The Fallow Deer at the Lonely House', published in 1922, which it might, conceivably, have influenced, although it must be admitted thet there are only superficial parallels: the setting is similar, but Hardy's mood is lyrical rather than sinister.

'The New House'

The 'House' was the one at Wick Green, specially built for Thomas and his family, and also the subject of 'Wind and Mist'. There, however, the gloomy premonition ('Sad days when the sun/Shone in vain') and the sad experience of the house is in the past. The poem is entirely typical of one side of Thomas's character and the obscurely motivated fear and pessimism that hung over much of his life. The wind joins his other great elementals, rain and darkness, with the same suggestion of infinity and human nothingness. He first used it in this connection in one of the sketches in *Rest and Unrest* which exactly expresses the feeling of the poem:

> The wind has as many voices as men have moods . . . Now it seems the youngest thing between earth and heaven, new made and fresh as bubbles on the brook. And now again it is an old wind, so old that it has forgotten everything except that it is old and that all other things among which it wanders are young and have changed and will change; and it mumbles fitfully that what is young now will in a moment be old, and that to be old is nothing, nothing.

For some remarks on this poem, see section 6.1, 'Form and rhythm'. Christopher Gillie (*Movements of English Literature*,

Cambridge, 1975) notes how the 'line-lengths vary, like the rise and fall of the wind itself', but perhaps it is the powerful rhythm which contributes most to the poem, with every last syllable, despite the enjambment, carrying a heavy stress.

'A Gentleman'

The dramatic, anecdotal quality of this poem contrasts with the more usual poems of personal reflection. Thomas's sympathies for the criminal are apparent in line 6, with its implication of the hypocrisy of those who criticise loudest, and in the humanity of the man's actions as described by the gipsy woman. (Thomas's early relations with Helen show his own liberal attitude on sexual matters.) The poem convincingly catches the speech of the gipsy:

> Now he was what I call a gentleman.
> He went along with Carrie.

Far from diminishing the poem's realism, the couplet form seems appropriate to its colloquial liveliness.

'When First'

Professor R. G. Thomas associates this poem with the summer of 1916, when Thomas left his study in the house built by his friend Geoffrey Lupton to go and live in the nearby village of Steep. Altogether, he had lived something like twelve years in this part of Hampshire. The poem expresses a middle-aged regret for the loss of hope and of youthful expectation of some surprising change in fortune. Hope has been replaced by a perception of the strength of the emotion of love, associated though it is with the pain of parting – love may be the profounder feeling, but it is also the more painful.

The poem is another example of the skill with which Thomas argues in verse, a far cry from any suggestion of Georgian naivety. Only a précis would do justice to the care with which he explains his state of mind, using his favourite octosyllabic line and confident enjambment. In the last verse, the metre drags and becomes more emphatic as Thomas declares the 'One thing' he knows.

'The Owl'

This is one óf Thomas's most anthologised pieces though, ironically, not one of his most typical: he consciously turns away from
self to express a view about the suffering of the soldier and the
beggar which seems to belong to an older poetic tradition. At the
same time, the reflection is very firmly rooted in the experience of
the first person and in no sense seems a forced moralisation. If not
the message, it is the rhythm which makes the first impression,
conveying the rise and fall of the speaking voice:

> Then at the inn I had food, fire, and rest . . .
> No merry note, nor cause of merriment . . .

The first six lines are marked by antithesis and balance: in the first
verse 'hungry' is set against 'starved', 'cold' against 'heat', 'tired'
against 'rest'. In the next two lines 'food, fire, and rest' are
balanced against 'hungry, cold, and tired'. But one of the most
striking features is the use of 'salted' in two senses: 'flavoured,
made better', but also 'made more bitter' – and Thomas honestly
admits to the first as well as the second.

'Melancholy'

Yearning for what cannot be attained, a sense of isolation and lack
of fulfilment, are characteristic of Thomas's poetry. His
melancholy is personal, rather than the result of some 'world-
sorrow' or unhappiness about the course of modern civilisation;
in this poem it seems a pleasant self-indulgence – comparable to
the wilful languor of Tennyson's Lotos Eaters' – and without the
bitter or sinister taste of a poem like 'Rain'. Thomas's pleasure in
melancholy ('naught did my despair/But sweeten the strange
sweetness') may be compared with Keats's claim in the 'Ode on
Melancholy' that those who most enjoy life are most aware of 'the
sadness of her [Melancholy's] might'. The imagery and the language ('raved', 'naught', 'cuckoo', 'dulcimers') suggest the influence
of the romantic poets. Repetition, the frequency of the 's' sound,
and instances of assonance contribute to the languid atmosphere.
The rhythm is especially striking, with the many long vowel sounds
(ay, ee, aw), underlining the poem's mood.

'The Glory'

The theme of dissatisfaction in the midst of happiness is also found in 'Ambition' (see below), which ends on this note. In Thomas's essay, 'The First of Spring', although it is a beautiful day, the central character feels a 'strong but vague and wordless desire to be something other than she was, to do something other than she was doing or had ever done – an unsatisfied desire', and Richard Jefferies's later writing is full of this sense of the unattainable:

> . . . The overwhelming thought that I shall not be able to penetrate [the sacredness of things] . . . that I shall not get at it; that I shall not conquer and make it human; that I shall not perhaps be able even to penetrate one little part of it.

In Walter de la Mare's poem, 'The Vacant Day', the poet finds his heart 'dumb/With praise no language could express' at the beauty of the summer's day, and looks in vain for its spiritual author. Only in the vaguest terms (line 13) does Thomas suggest a possible religious solution.

'The Glory' is one of Thomas's most effective monologues. Although its diction and syntax are elevated above prose, it carries the accent of the speaking voice. It begins with a verbless statement – the main clause is delayed for eight lines – the parenthesis consisting of a list of inspiring natural phenomena which ends with a 'metaphysical' surprise, 'The sublime vacancy/Of sky and meadow and forest *and my own heart* [my italics]. From statement the poem passes to questions, five in all, which gather increasing urgency as the conclusion is approached, and the poem ends on an audible note of unresolved frustration. The irregular rhyming echoes worry and unease. The rhythm is that of passionate thought, the heavy beats determined by the sense, not by pre-arranged pattern: compare the suppressed feeling of

> And tread the pale dust pitted with small dark drops

with the temporarily assuaging thought of

> As larks and swallows are perhaps with wings?

The last four lines show the influence of Keatsian diction ('oft', 'awhile', 'pent', 'naught') as the tone is still further heightened before the deliberate anticlimax of 'I cannot bite the day to the core'.

'Ambition'

The poem ends on a note of yearning, but unlike 'The Glory' most of it is filled with a full-blooded happiness. The sun, the wind (blowing from a hospitable direction), the soaring birds, and the smoke that assumes the shape of a 'motionless white bower/Of purest cloud' contribute to the sense of optimism. But few Thomas poems are without some shadow: the monosyllabic 'But the end fell like a bell' punctures the peace, and the poem closes on a note of uncertainty and vague dissatisfaction. The rhyme is irregular, and the feeling of naturalness, of coming 'straight from the heart', that the poem gives is further assisted by the enjambment which, even for Thomas, is remarkably disdainful of the limits of the line-unit. Lines 4–7 show four different parts of speech beginning each line and three different ones ending them; in line 2, the object of the previous line becomes the opening word, 'Ambition', while in line 17 the final word is the subject of the verb in the following line and the first word of the sentence to which it belongs. Despite this flexibility, the diction is in Thomas's more romantic manner – 'bower', 'twixt clouds and rime', 'twas' – and perhaps this, in the end, makes it less effective than some of the other monologues.

'The Sun Used to Shine'

The background to this poem is the meetings of Frost and Thomas in Herefordshire in the spring and summer of 1914. The relaxed tone of delivery contrasts with the darker imagery of war and the bitter-sweet flavour of the reminiscences. The fluency of the writing is remarkable: Thomas moves as easily from line to line, without end-stopping, as he does from verse to verse, giving the impression of the easy flow of memory. There are many suggestions of the imminent conflict, from the direct references in verses 3 and 4, to the 'sentry of dark betonies' and 'pale purple' crocuses from 'sunless Hades fields'. The poem ends with a magnificent coda, the broken statements suggesting the ebb and flow of the reflective mind, while the image of the tide is one of universal forces before which man is helpless.

'Sedge-Warblers'

As in 'The Glory', Thomas yearns for a still greater beauty than the one he actually experiences. However, in the poem's second sentence, he rejects this fantasy for the reality of nature itself:the sedge-warblers with their dissonant song represent this truth, and it is, presumably, this reality which they are 'Wisely reiterating endlessly'. The 'nymph' is a creature of his fantasy, like the classical figure whom he strives to imagine in *The South Country* (pp. 12–13) as representing the essential spirit of the English countryside. In a little known story by Thomas called 'A Sportsman Tale', a character objects when the classically-minded narrator 'used to discuss the Greek mythology and valiantly import the gods and goddesses and nymphs into our groves. Poetry was very well, but these figures in firm cold marble stood in no conceivable relation to any truth known to him'. Most of the poem is heavily laden with romantic diction and imagery, which is only thrown off when the sedge-warblers are introduced with their notes of sanity.

'Lob'

This appeared in the periodical *Form* in April 1916, and was one of the earliest of Thomas's poems to be published. In preparing material for his anthology, *This England*, Thomas came across much of the subject-matter that he used in 'Lob', which might be described as a hymn in praise of English folk-culture and an expression of his patriotism. Many pages of commentary could be devoted to explicating every allusion in the poem (Edna Longley gives 23 pages), but such assiduity is self-defeating where popular culture, not Miltonic scholarship, is the issue. Lob-like figures are to be found in Thomas's life and writing: 'Dad' Uzzell of Swindon was a colourful character whom he had met while on holiday there as a boy (*A Language Not To Be Betrayed, p. 250*), and another likely model was the old man in *The Country* (pp. 8–9) whom he encountered in the woods and recognised as a representative of English country-life which was passing away. One feature of the poem is its use of proper names: Thomas loved the quality of

English names of people and places – 'How goodly are the names hereabout!' he remarks in *The South Country* – and praised Hardy for utilising a device which aided 'reality by suggestion of gross and humble simplicity'. Thomas also wrote in his introduction to Isaac Taylor's *Words and Places* (London, 1911) that 'We shall not do well to make ourselves deaf to the ancient eloquence of names that can be as sweet to our ears as the laughter of Indian women long ago.'

The couplets in which the poem is written have the flavour of Chaucer, whose fourteenth-century verse is more reliant on end-stopping than is usually the case in Thomas. The editor Edward Garnett thought the style 'a little breathless or rough', but Thomas considered this effect appropriate and replied: 'I am doubtful about the chiselling you advise. It would be the easiest thing in the world to clean it all up . . . but it would not really improve it.' Unlike his more personal poems, in 'Lob' he writes in sentences that are often no more than two or three lines in length, delibe-rately avoiding what he praised Jefferies for also avoiding: 'It is deftness only that is wanting, and Jefferies was never deft'. Like Hopkins, who remarked that poetry was not 'itself' until spoken aloud (*Selected Prose*, ed. Roberts, Oxford, 1980, p. 137), Thomas believed that many difficulties could be overcome by sympathetic reading. He wrote:

If you *say* a couplet like

> If they had mowed [reaped] their dandelions and sold
> Them fairly, they could have afforded gold,

I believe it is no longer awkward. Then 'because' at the end of a line [line 16] looks awkward if one is accustomed to an exaggerated stress on the rhyme word which I don't think necessary.

'Tall Nettles'

'Lob's' sweeping perspective of English culture may be contrasted with the unassuming particularity of 'Tall Nettles', which fulfils the observation Thomas made about Francis Thompson, that 'Every one of his poems has this in common with great art that it lifts objects and ideas out of the dullness and weariness of blank acceptance in which we chiefly dwell' (Quoted in Longley, *A*

Language Not To Be Betrayed, pp. 49–50). There are several parallels in Thomas's prose where he also notes some unassuming farmyard scenes. The 'moral' of the poem, if so contrived a view can be taken of it, is that to the sensitive eye nothing in Nature is without its 'beauty'. For Hopkins this might be conveyed as inscape, and a poem like 'Inversnaid' with its cry of 'Long live the weeds and the wilderness yet' is a more dramatic representation of the same perception conveyed in 'Tall Nettles'. The poem suggests that the most trivial phenomena in Nature have a valuable part to play:

> I like the dust on nettles, never lost
> Except to prove the sweetness of a shower.

The last lines of 'What Will They Do?' use a similar image to imply the individual human being's value in the scheme of human relations.

Unassuming though the poem is, it is perfect in its way, the easy enjambment preventing the rhyme scheme from affecting the poem's sense of spontaneity. As C. Day Lewis wrote:

> The colloquial phrasing, the speaking cadences, the epithets few and unshowy; the quiet, almost diffident approach . . . nothing could be farther from the public epigram, nothing could sound less like an effort made to impress the country at large. (*Essays by Divers Hands*, vol. XXVIII, p. 76)

'First Known when Lost'

Like the previous poem, this one takes note of what would pass unobserved by many, and relates it in the tone of quiet reflection characteristic of Thomas. The woodman's destructive axe has made possible another creative insight, and although there are some awkward instances of poetic writing ('With a gleam as if flowers they had been') and the shorter lines and more concise syntax give a less fluent air than in 'Tall Nettles', the poem still wears its form loosely and speaks colloquially:

> I never had noticed it . . .
> And now I see as I look . . .

The lengthened-out last line imitates the sinuousness of the river it describes.

'In Memoriam (Easter, 1915)'

The poem underlines Thomas's tragic sense of the Great War in the months leading up to his enlistment in July 1915. Spring flowers, which might inspire traditional (and conventional) sentiment, become an image for the dead and their lost love. Flowers are lovers' gifts, are found at funerals, and in their *uncut* state here symbolise the young soldiers who have been cut down. In Wilfred Owen's 'Anthem for Doomed Youth' flowers are used as an image of the living's 'tenderness' for the memory of the dead, but even this evocative context can hardly match the power and richness of Thomas's use. His feeling and compassion are evident: as Jan Marsh writes: 'The poem is . . . touched with an entirely proper sentimentality' (*Edward Thomas, a Poet for his Country*, p. 149).

'Women He Liked'

The lanes around Steep may have given Thomas the inspiration for this poem: see Helen Thomas's remarks in the note to 'The Lane' (p. 27). It is one of Thomas's most poignant statements about melancholy, albeit expressed without emphasis or overt emotion. Bob tried to improve on Nature (out of his love for it), but failed, and his name remains ironically attached to the mud and gloom of the Lane. 'Liked' and 'loved' in lines one and three convey the comparative strength of Bob's feeling for women and horses respectively, like Fielding's Squire Western's for Sophia and his dogs in *Tom Jones*. Bob's failure might well have made the subject of a poem by Hardy, who would have discovered in it another example of the way events thwart man's intentions, but Thomas's treatment is compassionate:

> No one was to blame.
> To name a thing beloved man sometimes fails.

'To name' means to know and understand, and there may be a wealth of personal meaning, as Thomas recalls his own inability to plumb fully his feelings about nature.

The argument is presented in a remarkably logical and matter-of-fact fashion. The first verse gives a series of summary background statements. The second continues this, and begins the narrative ('All along the lane/He planted elms') which is recounted in the remainder of the poem: except for the key passage already quoted, Thomas refrains from all comment. The alternation of long and short sentence-lengths in the first three verses contrasts with the deliberately expansive final verse where the single sentence suggests the sweep of time and mortality (although, to be pedantic, it must be admitted that a comma hardly seems sufficient after 'gloom').

'As the Team's Head-Brass'

Thomas was resolving his own feelings about the war in this poem which was written while he was training at Hare Hall Camp in Essex. He eventually abandoned his 'safe' job as an instructor for a commission in the Royal Artillery which would take him to France. Like all the best conversation-pieces, it suggests more than the mere conversation says, so that while the personal and immediate war context offer significant levels of meaning there is, more fundamentally at issue, the permanence of the rural round and human love. In *Out of Battle* (London, 1972), Jon Silkin suggests that Thomas portrays the war as destroying the relationship between man and Nature, but more hopefully it can be suggested that the stoicism with which the ploughman continues his work and accepts his comrade's fate ('If we could see all all might seem good') is a positive quality, and the phrase 'the last time' has ominous overtones for the poet, not the general course of English rural life. The placing of the lovers entering, then emerging from the wood, at the beginning and end of the poem, particularly if the wood is seen as carrying the usual Thomas symbolism of death, is also a reminder that the forces of life are not so easily subdued.

Thomas may have read Hardy's poem 'In time of "the Breaking of Nations" ', which was first published early in 1916 and also attaches symbolic value to the agricultural round and human love. Hardy's stance, however, is more detached, 'philosophical' in the best tradition of the Victorian sage: he describes, then moralises, but unlike Thomas plays no personal part in the action. It is interesting that in praising another and earlier war-poem by Hardy, Thomas described it as an 'impersonal song', reflecting his own distrust of overt expression of patriotic feeling ('War Poetry' in Longley, *A Language not to be Betrayed*, pp. 131–5).

In the blank verse of this poem, Thomas comes as close as he ever did to reproducing the tones and syntactical forms of prose. The dialogue section seems to aim for complete authenticity, for which even Robert Frost, in a poem like 'The Hired Hand', did not strive. In the narrative passages, 'and' as the last word of a line shows Thomas's concern to resist any form of rhetorical exaggeration. But in the opening and final sections assonance and internal rhyme play an important part. Thus, in the first six lines, assonance on 'ah' regularly occurs, together with various forms of half-rhyme: 'bough', 'plough'; 'farrow', 'narrowing', 'yellow', which help to distinguish this passage from the more prosaic conversation that follows. The long sentence of the final lines, especially after the semi-colon, with its simple, often monosyllabic wording, and internal rhyme ('then', 'again', 'crumble', 'stumbling',), both imitates the action described and offers a sense of finality.

'Fifty Faggots'

By contrast with the dramatic nature of the previous poem, 'Fifty Faggots' is a soliloquy that also leads the speaker to the subject of the war. The faggots symbolise the uncertainty of life in general and of the poet's in particular. As with 'Tall Nettles', out of small beginnings, a poem evolves, carried on, it seems, in an undertone that eschews all emphasis and often chooses the language of common speech:

> Before they are done
> The war will have ended, many other things
> Have ended, maybe . . .

The poet writes 'Better they will never warm me' meaning perhaps that he has had his fair share of warmth from them already, by carrying them up.

'The Long Small Room'

One of Thomas's last poems, its enigmatic and somewhat sinister mood seems to show a man attempting to grasp the nature and purpose of his life. The house becomes his own life, and his writing hand operates compulsively from day to day without apparent achievement. A house was a powerful image for Thomas, as he demonstrates in 'The New House' and 'Wind and Mist', and he wrote in *The South Country* that a house 'beholds our sorrows and our joys. It is aware of birth, marriage and death'. Thomas admitted that the last line of the poem was abrupt, and if it has any clear connection with the rest of the poem, it seems to re-echo the idea of decay and death in the previous line. However, much can be forgiven for the imaginative power and clinical resonance of line 13, while on the second line Professor Longley remarks: 'the stanza itself "narrows up" from the spaced monosyllables and open vowels of its first line to the cluttered consonants of "fireplace filled" '.

'March'

Passages from Thomas's prose work, *In Pursuit of Spring*, are the basis for this poem, and suggest that he was following advice given by Frost, who said of Thomas in the period shortly before he began writing verse:

> Right at that moment he was writing as good poetry as anybody alive, but in prose form where it did not declare itself and gain him recognition. I referred him to paragraphs in his book *In Pursuit of Spring* and told him to write it in verse form in exactly the same cadence. That's all there was to it. (Quoted in Eckert, p. 150).

Compare lines 18–25 in the poem with the following from *In Pursuit of Spring*:

> All the thrushes of England sang at that hour, and against that background of myriads I heard two or three singing their frank, clear notes in a mad eagerness to have all done before dark . . .

A significant difference is that there is nothing in the prose corresponding to the two references (lines 16 and 28) to the thrushes 'knowing', a sentiment, perhaps, more appropriate to verse, and an indication of the liberation of Thomas's imagination in that form. The excitement of the thrushes' song is brilliantly evoked, but the feebleness of lines 7–9 and four separate uses of ' 'twas' are less successful.

'The Path'

There is a prose parallel in *The South Country* where Thomas describes a lonely Hampshire by-road circling down through the beeches from the downs above, but as with 'March' the poem carries richer overtones. The path represents the children's imaginative approach to life, which the adults – confined to the conventional road – cannot share, except vicariously. It is a path of 'silver', with no functional destination like a house or 'school'; its destination is 'legendary', which makes no sense in the cold light of reality.

More so even than 'The Combe', this poem achieves a remarkable atmosphere of mystery through the unerring artistry of the poet. It begins with a sentence in which the main clause is kept out of our sight until the final words. The three separate sections of the first half of the following sentence suggest, by their slight dislocation, the difficulty of looking down the slope, while the long unpunctuated passage from 'while' to 'bank' has a monotony of tone that reflects the dullness of adult vision. The simile in line 9 has the same value as the one in lines 20–21, both implying the greater 'truth' of the image rather than the real-life situation it describes. The path meanders in lines 8–12, but the half-line 'The children wear it' enables the poem to resume its logical direction. From line 17 we are taken almost to the end of the poem in one sentence as the eye follows the path's route, but there is an abrupt end as it reaches the light: 'sudden' and 'ends' (twice) with the half-rhyme and repetition underline the full stop.

'Words'

Thomas writes about the elusiveness of his craft. He had stated elsewhere: 'Words never consent to correspond exactly to any object unless, like scientific terms, they are first killed' (this recalls Wordsworth's "We murder to dissect"). And again: 'No man can decree the value of one word, unless it is his own invention; the value which it will have in his hands has been decreed by his own past, by the past of his race' (Quoted in full in Longley's edition, pp. 222ff). Thomas dramatises the difficulties of writing by personifying the words the poet uses. The very short lines of one or two stresses (perhaps sometimes three: 'You are light as dreams') and irregular rhyming suggest the elusiveness of language. The Welsh 'nightingales' in the last verse are the people of that country, for whom Thomas had a special affection.

'Rain'

In a single verse-paragraph, made up of two sentences, Thomas expresses a mood of love-death, the ultimate in melancholy: the rain does not bring happiness, yet it 'washes him clean'. The 'bleak hut' was at Hare Hall Camp, and the 'dead' and 'dying' no doubt include the soldiers mentioned in 'The Owl'. It seems paradoxical that Thomas should not wish for others an experience that he considers 'perfect' and 'cannot . . . disappoint', unless the stress falls on 'me' in the last line. The word 'rain/rains' occurs eight times in the poem, giving it an incantatory character. The mood is underlined by the heavy stresses:

> Rain, midnight rain, nothing but the wild rain
> . . . Blessed are the dead that the rain rains upon
> . . . Like a cold water, among broken reeds

The internal rhyme (again, rain, pain), assonance (bleak, me, remembering), and the frequency of 's' sounds create a disturbingly musical and persuasive picture of death.

Rain and its association with death is a theme that had a special significance for Thomas, in prose as well as in verse. *The Icknield Way* (pp. 280–3) has a powerful passage, quite unjustified by its context, in which rain becomes the ultimate absolute force and absorbs the writer into its finality. Rain has the same all-consuming power in *The South Country* (p. 280), and even in one of the very early essays it is associated with the idea of death: 'Even at the fireside I am washed by rain until I seem to glimmer and rejoice like the white headstone on the hill!' (*Rose Acre Papers*, London, 1904, p. 43).

Death had the same appeal to Keats, whose mood of melancholy pleasure at its anticipation in the 'Ode to a Nightingale' clearly appealed to Thomas:

> Darkling I listen; and, for many a time
> I have been half in love with easeful Death.
> . . . .
> Now more than ever seems it rich to die.

Writing about Keats, Thomas had significantly remarked that he could 'lie awake listening to the night rain 'with a sense of being drowned and rotted like a grain of wheat' ' (*Keats*, London, 1916, pp. 75–76). It is a theme which has continued to influence twentieth-century poets, and Alun Lewis, who was himself to meet a tragic end, and wrote of Thomas as his 'friend', recalled Thomas's death in the powerfully atmospheric poem 'All day it had rained'. He wrote too (in a context referring to Thomas): 'In my hand are four threads of death. When I talk of death I am talking of life. The first thread is love of death. It is a mood and seasonal as rain'. (Quoted in John Pikoulis, *Alun Lewis, a Life*, p. 116.)

'It Rains'

The parsley flower is the cue for memory, as is the herb Old Man, but in this case the recall is of a specific romantic episode, never to be repeated. Nevertheless, the memory makes the poet 'nearly as happy as possible' and he is able to console himself - there is still happiness to be found when he walks 'alone' in the rain (the confession is disarmingly honest and dispels any possible sentimentality). In the last four cryptic lines, it is the parsley flower which seems to hang almost without a stalk in the growing darkness, a symbol of the fragility of memory.

The poem, with its excess of 's' sounds and ease of enjambment, seems to whisper its message, and the transpositions of the usual sentence order ('there is none to break', further down to shake', and the last stanza) have the effect of slowing the verse and increasing the strangeness.

'The Brook'

The remark of a child sums up the poet's experience: a moment of intense vision, accompanied and induced by a registering of sensuous detail, of all that comes through 'sight and sound'. In such moments only the experience matters: 'All that I could lose/I lost', but unlike 'The Glory' there is no bitter-sweet afterthought to vex the poet. The preference for couplets over blank verse or irregular rhyme may have been determined by the role of the child which externalises, to some extent, the poet's personal experience.

'A Cat'

The point of the poem is that Nature has a place for the scavenger, as well as the singer. The first verse inspires pity for the cat, the second dislike, and the last is thoroughly ambiguous (although Thomas was no believer, the last line suggests his tolerance). Roland Mathias writes: 'The cat has a place in the scheme of things: the natural world contains both kindness and cruelty, right and counter-right, existing despite and yet because of each other. Edward Thomas accepted this, and did not romanticise.' (*Anglo-Welsh Review*, no. 26, 1960).

'Some Eyes Condemn'

Thomas criticised the sonnet-form because of its rigidity and impersonality, and this example (he wrote six in all) suggests it was not his most natural vehicle of expression. The eyes of the mistress are a conventional element in many Elizabethan sonnets:

> Love was the flame that fired me so near,
> The darts transpiercing were those crystal eyes. (Daniel)

Thomas's final exaggerated metaphor belongs to this tradition. There is flexibility, however, in the enjambment which cuts frequently across the rhyme-scheme, and there seems to be a touch of deliberate humour in the succession of verbs, 'rest, question, roll,/Dance, shoot.' Lines 10–12 presumably mean that some women whom he loved 'turned' away from him, bringing love to an end.

'Up in the Wind'

The poem is based on a prose version called 'The White Horse', dated November 1914, one month before the poem. (The White Horse is still an inn near Steep.) There is also an outline of it in Thomas's travel book, *The Isle of Wight*,' (1911) p. 29. This story of a young countrywoman drawn back partly unwillingly to her birthplace might have had a personal appeal for Thomas by presenting a lonely figure with complex attitudes toward her own place in life. Her stoicism, shared in their own way by the calves ('As careless of the wind as it is of us'), would also seem an admirable quality. An obvious companion poem to 'Wind and Mist', both are situation studies, in which Thomas examines the effect of the natural environment on character. Its superiority to the other poem is partly due to the well realised character of the girl, whose manner of speech has all the flavour of spoken English:

> Now I should like to see a good white horse
> Swing here, a really beautiful white horse.

'Wild', 'wildness' are key words as Thomas strives to recapture the strange appeal of the girl's situation,and the poem never becomes a merely naturalistic study. The long opening description is full of imaginative and idiosyncratic detail – the beech with its 'one bulging butt that's like a font', the common which 'calls itself' one

> because the bracken and gorse
> Still hold the hedge where plough and scythe have chased them.

Purely naturalistic detail, such as is found in his two Georgian contemporaries, Masefield and Wilfrid Gibson, is rare:

> the big saucepan lid
> Heaved as the cabbage bubbled.

'Cock-Crow'

The poem describes the transition from sleep to waking, fantasy to reality. Thomas's favourite image of the wood represents not only darkness, but the tangled growths of the unconscious, and the

shrill sound of the cock-crow in the waker's mind becomes identified with the cleansing power of daylight. The first three lines are made up entirely of monosyllables, imitating the beginning of a healthy return to normality. The cocks finally become heralds of the new day, which Thomas throws us into with appropriate abruptness in the last line. There is a fine analysis of the poem by F. R. Leavis in *Scrutiny*, Vol. XIII, Sep. 1945, pp. 132–4, who writes of the ending:

> The poet, aware as he wakes of the sound and the light together, has humoured himself in a half-waking dream-fantasy, which, when it has indulged itself to an unsustainable extreme of definiteness, suddenly has to yield to the recognition of reality.

'Adlestrop'

This much anthologised poem attempts to convey a moment of intense feeling, the poet's response to the total scene (of which the birds form only a part). The situation described is a remembered one, but it is a memory that brings happiness, not doubt or sadness.

Words can only be a lesser substitute for experience, and the more personal the experience the more uncertain the reaction of the individual reader. In this poem Thomas has deliberately refrained from *describing* his feelings, and presented instead the raw material – carefully organised – which gave rise to them. The poem has been criticised as 'self-indulgent' and failing to convey 'great or eternal truths' (Hyland, *York Notes*, p. 29), charges which do not seem particularly appropriate: as has already been suggested, the narrator remains virtually impersonal, while his 'message' is first and foremost the joy of the human heart's response to beauty. The poem is written in one of Thomas's favourite verse-forms, the four-line octosyllabic stanza rhyming *a b c b*: see p. 69 for some further discussion of this poem.

Adlestrop – a notably ugly name and an uncompromising title – is a village no longer served by a railway line and lies between Stow-on-the-Wold and Chipping Norton in Oxfordshire. Fragments of Thomas's personal writing, reprinted by Professor R. G. Thomas in his edition of the poems, clearly reflect the actual experiences on which the poem was based.

'Home'

This is one of three poems by Thomas under this title and describes his days at Hare Hall Camp in the spring of 1916. Thomas was beset by a perennial feeling of restlessness, psychological and spiritual in origin (although he contemptuously rejected a friend's advice that he should turn to the 'fat bosom of the church'). He sought his stability in self-knowledge and self-fulfilment, but he was more immediately influenced by the atmosphere of places where he lived and the sense of belonging given to him by his family. 'Home' tells us that he was deeply homesick away from these familiar surroundings and recognised the temporary nature of his friendship with the other men: it was this consciousness of the transitory character of army life that helped to make it bearable.

There is a certain stiffness about the writing of the poem, which is marked by inversion of word order and slight awkwardness of phrasing that seem to convey the barely controlled troubled feelings of the writer:

> Fair too was afternoon, and first to pass
> Were we . . .

> Between three counties far apart that lay
> We were divided and looked strangely each
> At the other . . .

'Celandine'

The poem examines the truthfulness of memory. The poet's first memory of the girl is both sad and unrealistic, but the sunlight on the celandines recalls the real (and attractive) person he had known. After a long account of her in the second verse, he declares that this, too, is not real, since it is no more than memory, but, in the last few lines, it is the smell of the flowers that acts as a guarantee of the authenticity of this memory (compare 'Old Man' where smell acts as a powerful trigger for memory). Thus the poet rejects a romantic fantasy, solely created by his imagination, in favour of a 'true' recall, authenticated by Nature. (In 'Sedge-

Warblers', Nature, through the birds, also helps the poet to reject
a private, nostalgic fantasy.)

'Old Man'

Writing to Harriet Monroe in January 1917 about a selection of
Thomas's verse, Robert Frost declared, ' "Old Man" is the flower
of the lot, isn't it?' and many later readers have echoed his
admiration. It is a poem in which memory plays a crucial part, at
first by anticipating what will be remembered, and then by
attempting to recall what remains ominously in the darkness of the
past. Making the same distinction as in 'Bob's Lane' between 'like'
and 'love' (see, too, lines 29–30), the poet insists on a feeling for
the herb Old Man which is beyond simple liking. He loves it as his
young daughter, now plucking it in the garden, will do some time
in the future, though she may forget the actual circumstances of this
particular day. He cannot remember (as she may not) when he
first smelt the scent, and all his efforts at recall end only in failure
and emptiness. The tone of the last eight lines is carefully created
to encourage a tragic reading of the poem: 'nothing', 'no', 'never'
and other forms of negation, often repeated, are verbally prominent; after a succession of clauses, there follows a series of
phrases, which culminate (still in the same sentence) in three
adjectives or adjectival phrases that emphasise the last impression
we must take – 'dark, nameless, without end'. Moreover, the
short clauses and phrases cause a rhythm full of heavy stresses,
which contrasts with the often colloquial quality of the preceding
part of the poem. The technique, as well as the meaning, does not
easily yield its secrets, and a number of paradoxes further express
this ambiguous character: the names of the plant partly express,
partly hide its nature; despite this objection, the poet likes the
names; on the other hand, he loves the herb, but does not like it;
finally, he does not like the smell, but would rather do without
others. We should also note that despite the absence of formal
rhyming, half-rhyme and assonance occur throughout the
poem – 'feathery', 'tree', 'rosemary'; 'snipping', 'tips', 'sniffs',
'clips'; 'mislaid', 'spray', 'wait'.
   A number of sources and parallels can be found in Thomas's
earlier work, including a prose version of the poem, some youthful
memories in *The Childhood of Edward Thomas* (pp. 15–16), and

an essay called 'Saved Time' (in the collection *Cloud Castle*) in which appears the idea of finding a key to the past, and so further understanding himself: in a dream the writer enters a room full of mysterious objects, and finally finds a chest which he seems to recognise as his. But he does not possess the right key and is told, 'Then you must wait until you have found the right one'. Professor R. G. Thomas has also discovered a revealing passage, dated one month before the poem, in one of Thomas's notebooks:

> Old Man scent, I smell again and again not really liking it but venerating it because it holds the secret of something of very long ago which I feel it may someday [*sic*] recall, but I have got no idea what. (*Collected Poems*, p. 381)

Whatever the final interpretation, it is clear that the genesis of the poem was deeply involved in Thomas's own experience and that its writing was part of his pursuit of self-knowledge.

'It Was Upon'

After apparently beginning in the present, the poem reveals itself as another exercise in memory. It was written at Hare Hall Camp in June 1916. 'A score years before' Thomas was studying for his Civil Service Examination (which he never took): the reference may be to the countryside around Swindon which was much visited by Thomas. The 'lattermath' is the second or later sowing after the first crop of the year, and it has been suggested that the last lines of the poem may refer to his uncertainty about the success of his poetry which had developed so late ('hoar' = delayed). The simpler explanation is that he is wondering about his fate in the war.

The sonnet form here (compare 'Some Eyes Condemn', *ante* p. 48) is perfectly adapted to Thomas's purpose: the octet describes the past, the sestet, the present, the whole of the poem encapsulating one related experience.

'Over the Hills'

This is another poem in which memory plays a crucial part. In the last six lines Thomas rejects the temptation to try to re-live past experience: he is the 'restless brook', and the image of the waterfall, the still lake, and the 'mountain's head' of stone represent the past's resistance to revival. There seems here to be some lingering nostalgia ('Recall/Was vain'), as well as acceptance. Rhyme is used with particular effect to express the mood of the poem. The first line has no corresponding rhyme; rhyme or half-rhyme then occurs irregularly until the last six lines when the patern is *a b a b c c*, suggesting that the misgivings and yearnings of the first 14 lines are now resolved into definite acceptance.

'October'

Inspired by autumn in Epping Forest, where he had been sent for rifle training, the first part of this poem is one of Thomas's most beautiful pieces of writing, though there is a characteristically dissatisfied conclusion: he suggests he could only fully respond to Nature's beauty if he were not the person he was or were simply an obedient part of creation, 'that has no time not to be gay'. Finally, however, he reflects that when he comes to look back from the future at this moment, he might well call it a time of happiness, rather than melancholy. In 'The Unknown Bird' Thomas in fact describes himself looking back to a time when he might have been unhappy, but recollection of the song of the bird brings him happiness: in both cases, memory transmutes experience. Another parallel is offered by 'The Glory' where Thomas is left dissatisfied by the beauty of the morning as he is by this October day.

The natural description is full of striking specific observation, such as

> the wind travels too light
> To shake the fallen birch leaves from the fern

as well as instances of Thomas's more detailed knowledge – scabious is a herb with coloured flowers, tormentil he describes elsewhere as a 'tiny yellow flower . . . a flat buttercup'. The importance of verbs should be noticed: the elm 'Lets leaves into the grass slip', the gossamers 'wander', the squirrels 'scold', giving an impression of life and activity, rather than a poetic set-piece. The sound of the poem is a very important part of its appeal, with a good deal of varied alliteration on g, l, s, w, and b, but comparatively little assonance. John Burrows in *Essays in*

Criticism, vol. VII, 1957, points out how 'October' particularly suggests the influence of the Odes of Keats: without discussing the detailed comparisons that Burrows makes, one must note the richness of the sensuous detail, the monologue form, and the narrator's ambivalent attitude toward melancholy.

'The Barn and the Down'

This is an anecdote of the power of illusion, arising directly from the poet's observation. Sometimes he has confused the barn for the down, at other times, trying to be more cautious, the down for the barn. He uses a powerful image in describing the down as

> A barn stored full to the ridge
> With black of night

but the poem has no pretensions to more ambitious objectives. Even so, the tightness of argument in so minor a poem is typical of Thomas.

'Wind and Mist'

Thomas is writing about the house that was built for him at Wick Green above Steep in 1909 (see pp. 10–11), where Myfanwy, his third child, was born (line 48). The same house figures in 'The New House', and Helen Thomas's account of it in *World Without End* (pp. 129–38) offers a similar gloomy picture. Just as in 'The New House', the wind carries profound personal overtones, and in lines 54–64 it symbolises the ultimate in human loneliness, a force that reduces man to a realisation of his own insignificance: 'My past and the past of the world were in the wind' is also the lesson of 'The New House'.

Running through the poem is the idea that the author chose the house as a refuge and retreat, but discovered, like the aesthete in Tennyson's 'Palace of Art', that a hermit cannot escape in this way from the natural consequences of his own humanity:

> I did not know it was the earth I loved
> Until I tried to live there in the clouds.

The error is that of the young man of inexperience, and the puzzling end of the poem, in which he says he would 'try the house once more', treats the unhappiness there as an inevitable mistake of youth.

Although 'Wind and Mist' consists almost entirely of dialogue between two characters, its dramatic form is incidental rather than fundamental. For Thomas it is a variation on the monologue, and the function of the stranger is to ask the necessary questions, rather than be developed as a character in a significant relationship. The difference can be seen by studying some of Frost's dramatic pieces in *North of Boston*, for example 'The Death of the Hired Man' or 'The Fear', where the participants involved are developed through their reactions to a particular situation.

'This is No Case of Petty Right or Wrong'

The poem was written in December 1915. What patriotism meant for him, Thomas had been revolving in his mind for the past year and more: the anthology, *This England*, essays written for *The English Review* and much reflection in letters and fragments show him developing a frankly territorial and social view of Englishness: English soil and English traditions, especially among the rural classes, were the values he was prepared to fight for. 'This is No Case' is his most outspoken defence of English values, a 'Lob' with exhortation and without the local detail. He has not to 'choose between the two' (the Kaiser and the typical English chauvinist) because his love for England is personal, not political, and 'justice and injustice' are abstract and irrelevant concepts. Unlike Sassoon and Owen he wishes for a post-war England that will be 'like her mother that died yesterday', and (lines 16–19) takes no interest in the historical causes of the war which later scholars will diagnose.

Thomas as critic took a poor view of most patriotic verse; he preferred the modesty and honesty of Coleridge's 'Fears in Solitude' which he described as 'one of the noblest of patriotic poems'. However, 'This is No Case' comes as near as any poem by Thomas to being strident, or at least positive, in its defence of the notion of fighting for one's country. The image of the phoenix is an awkward one, awkwardly expressed; on the other hand, the poem is at its best in the last seven lines where Thomas is at his most direct. It is also here that after the partly blank, partly rhymed verse of most of the poem, Thomas changes to rhyming couplets to underline the final message.

'Beauty'

In a state of depression, the poet is contemptuous of his own self-pity. He finds consolation in visualising a beautiful scene nearby, however, so demonstrating both the eternal appeal of nature and the survival within himself of a faculty always able to appreciate it. Thomas employs a fine image to describe the state of his own feelings in the depths of depression (lines 7–10), and the whole poem shows his control of the couplet form in expressing some of his most personal feelings.

'Liberty'

This is a powerful meditation on the dissatisfaction that Thomas felt with his own life, although its impact is somewhat marred by a difficult central passage. He describes his feeling of freedom as he witnesses a silent moonlit scene, but reflects that it is not true freedom where the individual concerned has no use to which to put it. The 'wiser others' are those hours when he has not been engaged in self-conscious reflection, and 'spent among' refers to the wasted hours of introspection. If these wasted hours could be recovered, he would be rich; he would also be rich if he could destroy them; 'poor' is ambiguous, since it means both that a large part of his life would therefore be taken away, and also perhaps that something valuable to his personality would be lost (this leads on to the statement that suffering is a necessary part of existence).

Keats's 'Ode to a Nightingale' is again an influence. The line 'And yet I still am half in love with pain' recalls Keats's 'I have been half in love with easeful Death'. The theme of life's bewildering complexity is also Keatsian: the critic Miriam Allott writes that the Ode 'expresses Keats's attempt to understand his feelings about the contrast between the ideal and actual and the close association of pain with pleasure' (*Poems of Keats*, 1970, p. 524). Although Thomas accepts this paradox in 'Liberty', the idea of death as a release from the pain of life is preferred in 'Rain' and 'Out in the Dark'.

The first six lines of the poem rhyme regularly, as if to paint the peaceful mood. Then follows an irregular mixture of rhyme and blank verse (perhaps to suggest Thomas's uncertainty). Finally, rhyming is resumed in the last six lines. Despite the syntactical awkwardness of the difficult passage already referred to, much of the poem still suggests the speaking voice:

> There's none less free than who
> Does nothing and has nothing else to do.

'Birds' Nests'

The poem is another example of Thomas's eye for the apparently insignificant (compare 'Tall Nettles' and 'First Known when Lost'), although he might also have known an essay by Jefferies, 'Birds' Nests', which describes the odd way in which nests are concealed and how, when the leaves fall, they appear 'in places never suspected' (*Field and Hedgerow*, London, 1948, pp. 283–4). The observation is delightful, and the tone unforced and unpretentious: the last lines will only seem an anticlimax to the reader who has assumed the inviolable convention that a poem ends with a moral; here, they are an entirely natural close.

'Home'

The 'one nationality' of line 4 is neither racial, nor political, but shared experience of the same place. It is familiar sights and sounds that make 'home', and for Thomas there is also, in the last lines, one of those characteristic moments of insight that put the final stamp on the experience. He uses an original verse-form: each stanza consists of 5 lines of four stresses each and one of two stresses, with one rhyme used in three alternate lines. In the last four lines of the last verse the alliteration on 's' and the hesitancy of the rhythm, especially in line three of this verse, give a sense of peace and silence.

'What Will They do?'

There seems to be a touch of self-pity, as well as contradiction, in this poem. Thomas first suggests that his friends can do without him when he is gone; then, he reflects that perhaps his friends need him, just as he needs them. In the last line, however, he seems to reject even that possible consolation. The image of the rain needing the flower is similar to the idea at the end of 'Tall Nettles' where rain and dust complement each other, so demonstrating that in Nature everything plays its part. This relative view of experience is also the conclusion to 'A Cat'. The poem is a good example of how naturally Thomas thinks in verse: it is not a thought of particular weight, perhaps personal to the point of triviality, but the two questions and their answers, the logical formulation of the argument ('It is plain that . . . ', 'But', 'Until') give the impression of a poet perfectly adjusted to his medium.

'Parting'

The poem was inspired by the departure of Thomas's son, Merfyn, to stay with Robert Frost in America, February 1915. Relations between father and son had been strained (see verse four, 'the ill it ended'). It is a difficult poem. It begins by saying that the past cannot be affected in any way by the present, that however much emotion was once stirred up, the past has now killed all emotion (it is not clear what Thomas means by 'Remembered joy', and so on). So there were two occasions of distress in his parting: firstly, the fact that it was a separation, secondly, that nothing could change the unhappiness it ended, which would now be imprisoned in the past. Hugh Underhill writes of this poem that it bears comparison with metaphysical verse: 'the lively speech-movement, the tendency towards involved and paradoxical thought, and something of an explorative habit accompanying a record of "the thought at the moment it arose in the mind" ' (*Essays in Criticism*, July 1973). Thomas's flexible use of the verse-form is shown by the number of enjambments from one verse to the next, by the varying length of the sentences (they increase as the poem goes on), and by the naturalness of the interjection in the last stanza, 'Not that, oh no!'

'Lights Out'

This is not, in fact, Thomas's last poem, although among the last (November 1916). He told Eleanor Farjeon that it was inspired by the 'trumpet-calls' that sounded 'all day' at the barracks in

Trowbridge (*The Last Four Years*, p. 219). 'Sleep' and 'forest' are common Thomas symbols for death: in his early book of essays, *Rose Acre Papers*, he speaks of sleep as a 'novitiate for the beyond', and in the poem 'The Dark Forest' he describes the forest as a place where

> . . . evermore mighty multitudes ride
> About, nor enter in;
> Of the other multitudes that dwell inside
> Never yet one was seen.

The poem is disturbing because it is about love of death, 'sleep that is sweeter/Than tasks most noble', and the poet is so desirous of it that,

> There is not any book
> Or face of dearest look
> That I would not turn from now
> To go into the unknown.

The desire to 'lose . . . myself' suggests the restless split-personality of 'The Other' longing for final 'release'.

The unusual and original verse-form reflects the strangeness of the theme. Each verse consists of one sentence – there is no run-over from one verse to another as in the previous poem – and although there is a great deal of formal, and sometimes striking, enjambment ('deep/Forest'), the short, heavily stressed lines and regular rhyming create an insistent rhythm. It is interesting that the poet Alun Lewis recalled 'Lights Out' when he went under anaesthetic for an operation: he wrote of an 'enveloping darkness . . . It was about two seconds in completely annihilating me – I surrendered to what Edward Thomas foresaw – the land he must enter and leave alone'.

The selection thus ends by reminding us of the complexity of Edward Thomas's personality and the careful artistry with which he expresses this in verse. Whatever interest or admiration we may feel for Thomas as a person, it is his poetry – and to a lesser extent his prose – which fully justifies the critical respect he now attracts, and which seems certain to continue for some time to come.

5 THEMES

5.1 THOMAS AND THE COUNTRYSIDE

When Thomas wrote that 'English poetry, at its best, can hardly avoid the open air', he said perhaps as much about himself, and his dependence on the countryside, as he did about English poetry. An acute and realistic observer of wild-life, trees, plants, country sights and smells, the weather and the seasons, and to a lesser extent country folk and their ways, he builds a picture of rural southern England which explains the patriotism that led him to fight in France. His eye is comprehensive and sees the most humble phenomena, the bird-dung, the broken-down farm machinery, the grass growing in old nests, as well as the more conventional beautiful morning and glorious sunset.

But although his work is full of natural observation, the latter's function is, in the final analysis, a means of self-expression, a reflection of the poet himself. An early reviewer, Robert Herring in the *London Mercury*, wrote that his poems are not so much about Nature as 'caused by a man's life among, or reactions to, Nature', and for some readers there is even a suggestion of claustrophobia rather than the open air: John Wain writes that in a landscape Thomas does not see God, but himself, and can 'study his own mind in the process of contemplation'.

No poem then is limited to mere description: the reader is invariably given an insight into the poet's state of mind. 'The Manor Farm' is first a concretely realised evocation of the scene, but finally a deeply felt expression of Thomas's patriotism. 'The

Brook' catches a transient, but piercing sense of beauty through a set of human and natural circumstances. In 'Celandine' the flowers become both a symbol of the girl he loved and a down-to-earth reminder to the poet that she no longer exists. Each of these poems is 'personal', but none of the experiences is necessarily limited to Thomas alone: like all the best lyric poetry, they may find an echo within the heart of the sensitive reader.

David Wright, in the Penguin edition of Thomas, describes him as one of the 'recorders and elegisers of the slow destruction of rural England and its culture by the industrial revolution and its consequences', and Jan Marsh has commented still more forcefully that he looked 'with contempt nurtured by Ruskin and Morris at everything urban and industrial'. These sweeping generalisations are arguably true of his prose works,but his verse remains obstinately elusive of doctrinaire assumptions: the eternal Lob will continue to be representative of rural values; 'shovel-bearded' Bob's failure to improve the Lane reflects Nature's stubborn resistance to human interference; Adlestrop's beauty is not injured by the train.

On the whole, Thomas avoids romanticising country values and indulging nostalgic regrets, although he was delighted by the somewhat self-indulgent rural writing of 'George Bourne' (George Sturt of Farnham in Surrey), especially by *The Bettesworth Book* (1901) with its idealistic account of the life and sayings of the author's old gardener, Bettesworth. The latter is seen as a representative, like Lob, of countless English country-folk, 'carrying on the work begun by their ancestors a thousand years ago'. But Thomas's lack of sentimentality avoids the easy 'philosophising' that 'Bourne' shows in a passage where he reflects on the probable fate of future Bettesworths: 'It seems as though destiny has decreed that this class of men, by centuries of incalculable and valiant endurance, should prepare England's soil not for themselves, but for the reaping machine and the jerry-builder.'

The impact of the countryside on Thomas goes deeper than the drawing of sociological conclusions, and provides the occasion for insights into experience which arouse feelings beyond the power of language to convey fully. Such are hinted at in 'The Glory', 'Ambition', 'The Unknown Bird', 'The Brook', and 'Often I had gone this way before'. These moments may be sad, or happy, or beyond such simple descriptions:

The men, the music piercing that solitude
And silence, told me truths I had not dreamed,
And have forgotten since their beauty passed. ('Tears')

Andrew Motion describes them as 'individual moods and intuitions hovering at the limit of articulation' and Thomas may have been thinking of these experiences when he wrote of the 'desire of impossible things which the poet alternately assuages and rouses again by poetry, in himself and in us'. It was appropriately in his introduction to a selection of essays by Jefferies, with whose mysticism he had such sympathy, that Thomas repeated from the philosopher William James the following definition of mysticism: 'States of insight into depths of truth unplumbed by the discursive intellect' – this is the intuitive 'knowledge' that the Sedge-Warblers so naturally sing,

> the small brown birds
> Wisely reiterating endlessly
> What no man learnt yet, in or out of school.

5.2 MEMORY

Reviewing the poetry of Walter de la Mare, one of his favourite writers, Thomas wrote that its atmosphere 'is like that of over-powering memory . . . He recalls things always drowned, softened, reduced, and with a more or less distinctly sad sense of remoteness'. Although this was written in 1912, before he began writing his own poetry, Thomas's dependence on memory is just as striking as de la Mare's; it differs, however, both structurally and atmospherically, is more deliberate in its use and more carefully organised in its contrasting of past and present.

'Yes, I remember Adlestrop', 'Was it but four years/Ago? or five?' ('The Unknown Bird'), 'try/Once more to think what it is I am remembering' ('Old Man'), 'Memory made/Parting today a double pain ('Parting'), and many more are instances of the unremitting pursuit in his verse of what R. G. Thomas calls 'the source of his own past happiness and sorrow'. The emotion involved is usually closer to the latter than the former, but again it is important not to overlook poems like 'Adlestrop' and 'The Unknown Bird' where memory brings strength and consolation.

The poems of memory broadly speaking follow one of two structures. In one, Thomas begins in the present, and then deliberately shifts to examine the past and attempts to effect some connection, as in 'The Unknown Bird' and 'Old Man' (where the attempt at recall fails). The reverse process also occurs, when the first lines are set in the past, as in 'It Was Upon' and 'Over the Hills', and the rest of the poem considers the original incident in the light of the present. Within these two extremes there is much variation: Thomas, as he wrote of Lafcadio Hearn, 'more than any other man . . . appears to have been unable to forget "the dark backward and abyss of his own immemorial past", not in order to dwell on it, but as a means to take stock of his own present. Nostalgia, in any loose sense, does not seem the right description for this attitude, but in an article in *Scrutiny* in May 1932, D. W. Harding defined the term as a yearning for one's home or group, and hence a sense of 'not belonging'. Such a feeling of alienation, though personal rather than social, seems an accurate description of Thomas's own situation: it is with this that his poetry attempts in all honesty to come to grips, and does so almost entirely without self-pity.

5.3 MELANCHOLY

Thomas's poem of this name stresses the complex nature of melancholy: he fears solitude, but 'far more' he fears 'all company'; he desires what he knows to be unattainable, yet his despair 'sweetens' what he feels. The poem's restrained rhythm and the many 's' sounds suggest a weary passivity that weakens the poet's attachment to life:

softer and remote as if in history,
Rumours of what had touched my friends, my foes, or me.

Tennyson paints the same atmosphere in 'The Lotos-Eaters', where Ulysses's men surrender to the languor of the island, and the reality of their previous life loses its hold. Thomas recognises that melancholy is both attractive and destructive, and as Keats pointed out in his 'Ode', may be inspired by the experience of anything that is beautiful, and hence subject to human decay.

In 'October', Thomas's experience of beauty leads him to regret his own tortured humanity:

> now I might
> As happy be as earth is beautiful,
> Were I some other or with earth could turn.

But his pessimism is finally halted by the consoling, if devious reflection that looking back from the future, he may recall the day as a happy one:

> And this mood by the name of melancholy
> Shall no more blackened and obscurèd be.

(This experience actually happens in 'The Unknown Bird'.)

Other aspects of Thomas's melancholy are not necessarily limited to poems where the word is actually used. 'Rain' speaks of a 'love of death' as love of something which is 'perfect' and 'Cannot, the tempest tells me, disappoint'. 'Lights Out' similarly finds death, symbolically identified with the dark forest, offering 'sleep that is sweeter/Than tasks most noble'. 'Out in the Dark', in its last verse, suggests the equal attraction of life and death.

In other poems, Thomas reveals a cast of thought which tends towards melancholy: the confession of inadequacy in 'And You, Helen'; regret over the passing of a happy past ('The Sun Used to Shine'); regret that the past cannot be relived ('Over the Hills'); morbid consciousness of a dual-self ('The Other'), and more, but it is a peculiarly incomplete view of Thomas to see him as dominated by gloom and despondency. 'Adlestrop', 'The Brook', 'Manor Farm' celebrate intense moments of happiness; 'Tall Nettles' and 'First Known when Lost' find beauty and 'inscape' in the least regarded aspects of nature; 'Lob' affirms the vigour of English tradition. The story of Thomas's life reveals the moods of deep depression to which he was subject, as well as much joy, and his poetry fairly reflects the emotional extremes of this complex man.

5.4 WAR

If a war poet is one whose poetry is mainly about, or at its most effective in dealing with war, Thomas hardly qualifies for the description. Only about half a dozen poems in R. S. Thomas's selection make any reference to the war, and even if the rest of his work is taken into account, it would still be misleading to talk of him in the same breath as Wilfred Owen or Siegfried Sassoon. For them, the experience of war was traumatic and overwhelming, and totally absorbed their poet's instinct, whereas Thomas was at the Front only two months and an artilleryman, not an infantryman in the trenches. Even had he been there longer, as someone who was already into middle age, it is unlikely that he would have responded in the same way as younger men.

If, however, the term 'war poet' can be more loosely used to describe anyone whose poetry from time to time shows an awareness of the conflict, recognising its implications as both a public and personal tragedy, Thomas is entitled to the name. At one extreme, his 'This is No Case of Petty Right or Wrong' is (for him) a surprisingly explicit affirmation of patriotic values, although based on grounds far from jingoistic – the jingo would not have been pleased at the Kaiser being called a 'god' compared with 'one fat patriot', or with Thomas's refusal to arbitrate on the justice of the cause.

Very different is the restraint of 'As the Team's Head-Brass' which develops Thomas's concern over the war through a naturalistically observed scene. The poet's feelings about going to the Front, and the war's local effect, are the subject of casual conversation as the plough sweeps up and down, yet these details seem to encapsulate a whole tragic vision of individual man as victim of circumstances beyond his control. The most positive aspect of the picture is the lovers, who represent the will to live, although Thomas, in harmony with the mood of the poem, leaves the reader to draw this more optimistic conclusion. In 'The Owl' Thomas speaks on behalf not just of soldiers, but of all the suffering. Two of his most direct poems about the war are also among his shortest, the wryly ironic 'A Private' and 'In Memoriam (Easter 1915)', with its moving image of unpicked wild flowers recalling the dead young men who will never pick them for their 'sweethearts'.

But Thomas's best poetry is where he is most personal and where the war is one element in the private feelings he describes. 'Rain', similar to 'The Owl' as a 'prayer' for the dying and lonely inspired by Nature, is first of all a confession of his death-loving melancholy. The beautifully caught reflectiveness of 'Fifty Fag-gots' sees war, as in 'As the Team's Head-Brass', in terms of all the forces which make the poet's future unpredictable. 'The Sun Used to Shine' takes powerful note of the 'rumours of the war remote', but is also an elegy to friendship and a celebration of the nostalgic strength of memory.

Taking these and certain other poems into account, one may agree with Alun Lewis's verdict that the War became for Thomas 'an integral part of his life experience, not a violent thought-slaying wound as it was to Owen'.

6 TECHNICAL FEATURES

6.1 FORM AND RHYTHM

> Classical forms of poetry are a rough approximation which can never mould the thought . . . Every poetical work calls for its own particular rhythm – a rhythm in the whole, a rhythm in the parts, and a rhythm in the paragraphs and sentences. Regular line-cadence is good: but it's the infancy of poetry: it checks poetry, and breaks it up into fragments – A literary piece, if it is really felt and expressed, should be like a piece of music, with shades of emphasis, silences, themes, an over-all harmony, &c . . . – a completely individual typographic arrangement. (Teilhard de Chardin, *The Making of a Mind*, trans. René Hague, London, 1965).

One aspect of Thomas's originality is reflected in the variety of forms which he chose to express his individual vision. Brevity, however, tends to be the rule, and, with notable exceptions, few of his poems exceed 30 lines in length. He explained: 'I try not to be too long – I even have an ambition to keep under 12 lines'. And more revealingly, in his book about Maeterlinck, the Belgian playwright: 'Anything, however small, may make a poem; nothing, however great, is certain to. Concentration, intensity of mood, is the one necessary condition in the poet and in the poem'.

'Adlestrop' is not the shortest of his poems, but it suggests a careful organisation of lines and verses to produce its unique effect. A comparatively regular form of four-line octosyllabic verses controls what could have been an intolerably diffuse experience – the expression of a sense of beauty or ecstasy. The rhyming of the second and fourth lines acts as a measure of restraint, although in reading the poem, the enjambment makes the rhyme only just perceptible. The short sentences of the first two verses admirably represent the matter-of-factness of the poet's first impressions, acting as a contrast to the two extended sentences which follow and respectively occupy each of the remaining verses. 'And' becomes a crucial word as Thomas builds up the total experience to its climax (the diction and syntax are also elevated). The speech rhythms of the opening verses take on a less flexible, more declamatory quality in the last two stanzas:

> And willows, willow-herb, and grass,
> And meadowsweet, and haycocks dry.

The internal rhyming plays an important part in the structuring of the poem. The early use of 'name' in line 2 anticipates the rhyme of 'came' and 'name' in the second verse; 'dry' and 'sky' link with 'high' and 'by'; and in the last verse the final syllable of 'mistier' finds four rhymes.

Regular, set forms were anathema to Thomas, from a conviction that they encouraged poetic insincerity. As he told a friend, Jesse Berridge, himself a minor poet:

> Personally, I have a dread of the sonnet. It must contain 14 lines, and a man must be a tremendous poet or a cold mathematician if he can accommodate his thoughts to such a condition

and he complained that the sonnet form encouraged Berridge to 'use words loosely, to forget that words have a value beyond their sound'. To expect that every poem by Thomas should be a successful demonstration of imitative form, reflecting in its shape and structure the experience it describes, is to ask for more than any poet could provide, but instances of his care in the choice of line and stanza form are many. In 'The New House' the structure and shaping is part of the poem's uneasiness: long and short lines alternate, and there is some variation in the number of heavy stresses. The occurrence of enjambment and end-stopped lines is unpredictable, yet the concluding word to each line is usually an important one. Certain rhetorical effects are also employed at the beginning and end of lines: in lines 5 and 6, 'Old', the keyword, is placed in two crucial positions. Similarly, in line 13, 'All' and 'naught' are balanced against each other.

But perhaps most characteristic are the blank verse or irregularly rhymed monologues, where we seem to be reading, as Andrew Motion writes, 'a mind actually engaged in the act of thinking'. Diction and syntax vary from the colloquial to the 'poetic', but the tone is that of the thoughtful man, meditating to himself: the metrical foot and the line come second in importance to the sentence and the paragraph. The second sentence of 'Liberty' extends over nearly six lines, the fifth over eight, with some daring enjambment – the subject 'I' at the end of line seven, 'among' at the end of line sixteen. In the irregularly rhyming 'The Glory', the long soaring opening sentence is followed first by a question extending over eight lines, and then by a series of shorter ones (with starting-points at different places in the line), until a final short categoric statement brings the poem to its conclusion.

The freedom of Thomas's enjambment is equally notable in rhymed couplets, where he sometimes places the verb's subject or the attributive adjective at the end of the previous line. In 'The Other', for example, 'A customer, then the landlady/Stared at me', and 'dark impossible/Cloud-towers': the insistent rhyme, however, prevents the complete ascendancy of the enjambment, and creates a tension at a technical level which contributes to the strange atmosphere of the whole poem.

'It Was Upon' is one of Thomas's rare sonnets and demonstrates the flexibility with which he can deal with a set form. This is principally achieved by managing a series of short statements in the octet to contrast with the single sentence that makes up the last six lines. The curtness of these statements is emphasised by four of the six sentences in the octet ending at the caesura. A contrast is thus created between the past (the octet) and the present (the sestet).

No reader of Thomas can fail to note his use of such devices as half- (or consonant) rhyme, internal rhyme, and repetition. 'Old Man' begins by repeating 'Old Man or Lad's Love' in reverse order (in the poem youth and age are seen as inevitably linked in the round of time) and ends with the phrase carrying ominous echoes of human insignificance. 'Name', mentioned in line one, appears thrice more in the brief opening section, each time in the stressed final position, and is picked up again conclusively in the last line as 'nameless', as the poet admits his failure to interpret the experience. Other keywords may be identified by the reader.

'The Combe', with its keyword 'ancient', is bound together by an intricate system of alliteration, assonance and internal rhyme ('bramble', 'scramble'). The b's ('bramble', 'briar', 'beech', 'bird', 'badger', 'Briton', 'beast') are all nouns that help to convey the substance of Englishness. The 'ah' sound is repeated several times, 'dark', 'half', 'far'; while 'yew', 'juniper', 'roots', 'moon' provide more instances of chiming in the poem.

Although Thomas's poetry is often described as unassuming, his art can never be underestimated. He was a conscious artist, and no poem of his, however unpretentious in content, fails to demonstrate his concern to answer the challenge of form and technique.

6.2 SYNTAX AND DICTION

As a poet, partly through his own literary experience, partly through the encouragement of Robert Frost, Thomas adopted a language that used both the traditional vocabulary of poetry and the more informal speech of the educated man. Examples of the latter can be found in most of his poems:

No one saw him: I alone could hear him ('The Unknown Bird')

> Now first, as I shut the door,
> I was alone ('The New House')

> She found the celandines of February
> Always before us all ('Celandine')

'The Manor Farm' shows a characteristic mixture of the informal and 'poetic'. It begins in a language and syntax in which only 'rills' strikes a literary note:

> The rock-like mud unfroze a little and rills
> Ran and sparkled down each side of the road
> Under the catkins wagging in the hedge.

Against this attractive matter-of-factness Thomas sets the following:

> But earth would have her sleep out, spite of the sun;
> Nor did I value that thin gilding beam
> More than a pretty February thing.

The personification, 'have her sleep out', 'spite of', 'Nor did I value', 'gilding' belong to a different, more romantic mode of writing, giving the poem a place in both the English past and present. The language of the poem's coda, 'The Winter's cheek flushed . . .' is appropriate to the assertion of age-old English values, even if many readers may feel unhappy at the excess of Keatsian personification.

'The Path' begins on a Miltonic note, with its delayed main clause and contrived syntax of 'saves from' in the second line,

> Running along a bank, a parapet
> That saves from the precipitous wood below
> The level road, there is a path,

and like Milton, Thomas exploits a phrase of plain English as a contrast:

> They have flattened the bank
> On top.

The desire for absolute honesty sometimes led Thomas to adopting argumentative structures which have rightly been compared to the logic-chopping of the metaphysical poets:

> There's none less free than who
> Does nothing and has nothing else to do,

> Being free only for what is not to his mind,
> And nothing is to his mind. ('Liberty')

There are also passages where Thomas is difficult simply because
he has not worried the thought into its most intelligible form.
Stanza nine of 'The Other', 'Once the name I gave to hours', can
only be half-defended on the grounds that its 'syntax exactly
reproduces the poet's psychological mystery tour', especially when
the same critic (Professor Langley) has to confess: 'The direction
and conclusion of the sentence itself are hard to "guess" '. Nevertheless, it is true that ambiguity and ambivalence exist in Thomas's
work as an honest reflection of his own genuine questioning and
uncertainty; seen in this light, such passages are further evidence
of the authenticity with which he conveys his personal feelings in
verse.

   Much of Thomas's poetry, even where the diction is far from
prosaic or the thought is tightly argued, reflects the tone of the
speaking voice or, where applicable, the meditating consciousness.
There is some rhetorical strain about the lines from 'Liberty'
quoted above – for example, 'none' for 'no one who is', 'who' for
'the person who' – but read dramatically, as if one were the
meditating poet, with proper regard for pause and emphasis, the
lines have a wry, but natural tone which is authentic Thomas:

> There's none˘ less frée than whó
> Does nóthing//and has nóthing else to dó,
> Being freé//ónly for what is nót to his mínd,
> And nóthing ĭs to his mínd.

Thomas particularly admired Frost's use of plain speech in the
volume *North of Boston*, praising the poems because the language
was 'free from the poetical words and forms that are the chief
material of secondary poets'. He was also impressed by the
liberality with which Frost interpreted this Wordsworthian
approach: 'He has not the least objection to any vocabulary
whatever or any inversion or variation from the customary gram-
matical forms of talk'.

Thus, with the example of Frost, and to some extent Hardy to fall back on, as well as the conclusions of his own literary experience, Thomas took a catholic view of the range of diction available to poetry, provided that in his choice, the poet was sensitive to what Frost called the 'sentence-sounds', or feeling of the natural speaking voice. In the Georgian poet, Lascelles Abercrombie, whom Thomas came to know during the holiday with the Frosts in Herefordshire in the summer of 1914, Thomas found another fellow-spirit. Abercrombie believed that 'the main thing necessary for the poet's art is the living mode of speech he hears commonly about him' (*Poetry and Contemporary Speech*, Feb. 1914), but claimed, nevertheless that all of the English language, traditional as well as modern, should be available for the poet to draw on. Thomas was similarly undoctrinaire, for critical as he was of the unnaturalness of the language of writers like Walter Pater, he freely admitted that 'much good poetry is far from the speech of any men now'.

6.3 IMAGERY AND SYMBOL

In its widest meaning, the term 'imagery' may be applied to all the sense phenomena which appear in a poem and are the expression in concrete terms of the poet's experience. In this meaning, the world of Nature provides much of Thomas's imagery, for as he himself wrote of Richard Jefferies, he 'could not uncover his soul without [the countryside]'. In its more usual, and restricted sense, it is applied to all those figures of speech – similes, metaphors, personification, and so on – which are employed by the poet's imagination to intensify the experience presented in the poem. It is in this sense, that the word will be discussed here, in its application to Thomas's verse.

Since Thomas's ideal was a poetry free from rhetoric and as close as possible to the intonations of the speaking voice, the role of imagery in his verse is less conspicuous than in many poets. In Thomas the image does not dominate the poem nor, with certain exceptions, does it provide the central meaning of the poem. Nevertheless, examples of original and striking imagery may be found: the poet's writing hand 'crawling crab-like over the clean white page' in 'The Long Small Room' is a picture of creative futility as macabre as Eliot's 'pair of ragged claws scuttling across the floors of silent seas'. Equally disturbing in its mixture of the cosily rural and the infinite is the cry of the Unknown Bird, 'As if a cock crowed past the edge of the world', reminiscent of Arnold's *Dover Beach*, where the Sea of Faith retreats 'down the vast edges drear/And naked shingles of the world'.

His most moving simile is the prayer for the suffering in 'Rain':

> Helpless among the living and the dead,
> Like a cold water among broken reeds,
> Myriads of broken reeds all still and stiff.

The repetition, assonance, and half-rhyme lend the passage a particular and disturbing power, which is also found in poems with a more explicit reference to the First World War. In the idyllic 'The Sun Used to Shine', the sinister images of 'sentry of dark betonies' and 'sunless Hades' (one of Thomas's rare classical allusions) are deliberate intrusions on the nostalgia evoked by past and happy times.

'Over the Hills' concludes magnificently with an extended image that defines the irrecoverability of the past:

> . . . no more could the restless brook
> Ever turn back and climb the waterfall
> To the lake that rests and stirs not in its nook,
> As in the hollow of the collar-bone
> Under the mountain's head of rush and stone.

Only the two final monosyllabic nouns bring a sudden conclusion to the powerful drive of these lines, as memory realises its impotence.

Simpler effects are achieved elsewhere. The disorderly trail of hounds in 'Tears' becomes a 'great dragon', suggesting both the romantic and sinister aspects of the experience. In appropriate rural imagery, Farmer Hayward is 'like a cob' and the old man's face in 'Lob' as 'sweet as any nut'. Less fortunately, in 'Melancholy', rain falls 'soft as dulcimers', which recalls the exotic 'Kubla Khan' rather than the homely English countryside. One of Thomas's best remembered lines is the metaphor which concludes 'The Glory': 'I cannot bite the day to the core', where the connection of 'bite' and 'day' has the quality of metaphysical wit.

Certain key images in Thomas's writing take on the function of symbols: forests, darkness, sleep, rain, roads and paths become powerful metaphors. In 'Out in the Dark', where darkness moves quicker than the 'swiftest hound', Thomas describes the power and fascination of death. The wind of 'The New House' and 'Wind and Mist' is an image both of human mortality and Nature's implacability. Rain is an annihilating force, washing him 'cleaner' than he has been 'Since I was born'. The forest is dark, but it also offers secrecy and protection:

> The forest foxglove is purple, the marguerite
> Outside is gold and white,
> Nor can those that pluck either blossom greet
> The others, day or night. ('The Dark Forest')

All these examples reflect the essentially tragic tendency of Thomas's imagination and a man who, while curious of life, was still more fascinated by the mystery of death.

7 CRITICAL RECEPTION

7 **CRITICAL RECEPTION**

C. H. Sisson's claim in 1981 that Thomas had now become 'the centre of marked academic attention' is evidence of the slow climb to critical acclaim that the poetry had achieved in the 60 years since Thomas's death. The enthusiastic pages by F. R. Leavis in *New Bearings* in 1932 bore no obvious fruit, and during the thirties and forties Thomas's poetry seemed to vanish from the shelves of the critics.

Thomas had not wanted easy popularity, and his first poems had appeared under the pseudonym of Edward Eastaway because he wished to avoid being judged in the light of his previous career as a prose writer. Only on his death at Arras did his identity become generally known. *Poems* came out under his own name in October 1917, and in the following year *Last Poems* brought the remainder of his work to the public. The reception was appreciative in some quarters, but, seen with hindsight, disappointing in its limitations.

The popular Irish poetess, Katherine Tynan, writing in *The Bookman* about a selection of 'Edward Eastaway's' verse that had appeared in *An Annual of New Poetry* (March 1917), reported that in his poetry alone was to be found 'the thrill, the surprise. Others of the poets in this anthology give us beauty, but it is an expected and customary beauty, whereas this one is new'. The *Times Literary Supplement* quoted his work at length, but spent a good deal of space regretting what it considered an excess of description at the expense of a philosophy. Still, the reviewer thought he was a 'real poet, with the truth in him'. In a later review the same periodical called his poems 'among the rarest fruits of these strange years', and noted prophetically that 'What is uncustomary, especially in art and in literature, must slowly win its way'.

Writing in the *New Statesman*, Sir John Squire, who was to become the doyen of anti-modernist critics, was prepared to grant him a place 'among the lesser English poets', and three years later, in 1920, in a collection of his essays, gave Thomas higher praise, particularly for the 'closeness of his observation and the use he made of the ordinary'. The poet Walter de la Mare, who was a personal friend of Thomas, wrote two pieces about him, the first an appreciative review in April 1917 in the *Saturday Westminster Gazette*, and the second, and better known, an introduction to the 1920 edition of Thomas's *Collected Poems*, where he remarked that 'like every other individual writer, he [Thomas] had un-learned all literary influences', a perceptive tribute to Thomas's revolt against poetic rhetoric.

Other appreciative reviews during the first three years after his poetry appeared, came from Edward Shanks, John Freeman, Middleton Murry, and Desmond MacCarthy, but most of these implied the minority appeal of his work, and only Middleton Murry in this group could be identified with some of the more modern attitudes in criticism. One looks in vain for notice of Thomas by the avantgarde, the Eliot camp or, later, the 'new' criticism associated with I. A. Richards: for these writers he was irretrievably lost in Georgian backwaters. The quality of his genuine originality was not extreme enough to place him with the acknowledged moderns, but it was enough to distance him from orthodox Georgians. The championship of such traditionalists as Walter de la Mare and Edward Garnett was too modest and too limited to effect any change in literary opinion throughout the 1920s.

In 1932 in *New Bearings*, F. R. Leavis made a unique contribution to Thomas's reputation by welcoming him – more or less as he welcomed Gerard Manley Hopkins in the same volume – as a 'representative modern sensibility' and rejecting the Georgian connections. He underlined the highly personal character of his writing about Nature and spoke of the 'inner life which the sensory impressions are notation for', praising the precision of his description and his 'sincerity'. Today these pages are still required reading on Thomas, but in the thirties they appeared to make no impression on the current lack of interest in his poetry, although biographical studies by his wife Helen, the American scholar Robert Eckert, and by John Moore suggested the existence of a select group of admirers.

In 1947, William York Tindall, in *Forces in Modern British Literature*, continued to see him as a Georgian: 'Farmers, barns, flowers, the open road attracted Thomas's accurate eye, inspiring quiet verse, better than most in this kind'. The first sign of a general change in attitude to Thomas was the half-dozen pages devoted to him in John Lehmann's *The Open Night* (1952). The author noted the interrelationship of pleasure and pain and the attempt towards exploring an 'apprehension beyond words' in verse that was both sincere and unpretentious. In a lecture delivered in 1954, but not printed until 1956 (see 'Further Reading'), the poet C. Day Lewis was also impressed by Thomas's 'extraordinarily honest kind of poetry' and his rhythmic variety. He remarked that Thomas's 'lack of wholeheartedness – of passion, if you like – is what chiefly limited him and kept him a minor poet, just as it is this honesty which made him such a good poet'. He concluded that Thomas's unhappiness arose from the 'limitations of life itself': 'Nothing less than God, we might say, could have given peace . . . to that kind of man'.

Edward Thomas by H. Coombes in 1956 was the first full-length study, although much of it was devoted to Thomas's prose. Coombes remarked on the relative immaturity of Thomas's sense of dissatisfaction, but added, of his verse, that 'if we say it is minor poetry, it is chiefly because his range is limited'. Roland Mathias, in the *Anglo-Welsh Review* (1960), also noted this lack of a sense of fulfilment and associated it with a sort of fatalism: 'Thomas wanted to be happy, but did not know how to be because there were no verities which did not change'.

The poet Vernon Scannell's pamphlet for the British Council in 1963 (see 'Further Reading') began by referring to the recent rise to 'critical acclaim' of Thomas's work, and argued that his reputation had been held back because he did not belong to the intellectual tradition of Pound and Eliot. Like Lewis, he noted the apparent gap created by the absence of religion in his life, and saw running through his poems a 'deep nostalgia for an idealised personal and historical past, which, in Christian terms, would be interpreted as the desolation consequent upon the sense of separation from God'.

An early piece of work by Professor R. G. Thomas on his namesake appeared in 1968. Professor Thomas can now (1987) rightly be called the foremost authority on the poet, and then, as now, he insisted on the 'underlying unity of all the prose and poetry that Edward Thomas had written' ('Edward Thomas, Poet and Critic', in *Essays and Studies*, vol. 21, London, 1968). He has also continued to be sceptical of the extent to which the war and Robert Frost were responsible for Thomas writing poetry; in his opinion, Thomas, through a process of maturity, had become a poet by 1914, and external causes provided no more than the final stimulus. In his book on Thomas in the *Writers of Wales* series a few years later, Professor Thomas wrote of the advantages of a chronological reading of the poems for evidence of a 'dramatic development in skill, self-assurance, and versatile adaptability to the new rhythms that, so [Thomas] thought, were to be found in his verse but had long been absent from his prose'.

Both William Cooke's *Edward Thomas, a Critical Biography* (1970) and C. H. Sisson's *English Poetry, 1900–1950* (1971, with a Postscript, 1981) treat him as one of the most important of twentieth-century poets. Cooke was particularly interested in rehabilitating Thomas as a war poet and concluded that ' "the pity of war" entered Thomas's poetry before Owen had even enlisted'. Sisson pointed out that unlike the youthful Owen, Thomas had become a soldier with nearly 40 years of his life behind him, which tended to diminish the immediate impact of the war upon him. Sisson declared, however: 'I would say that fifty years have not given him his rightful place. He is, without doubt, one of the most profound poets of the century'.

Edna Longley's more or less complete edition of the poems in 1973, together with a comprehensive commentary, must have encouraged a great deal of work on Thomas, judging by the rush of articles in academic periodicals over the next ten years. Critics were interested not only in his writing, but also in his literary context, and the poetry of Hardy became a popular parallel. Maire Quinn in the *Critical Quarterly*, Spring 1974, spoke of Hardy's 'assertion of the value of the past' which was alien to the more sceptical and 'distinctively modern sensibility' of Thomas. J. Dollimore in the same journal (Autumn 1975) considered how the two poets made use of the external world, which in Thomas's case was ultimately ungraspable in its significance. While Christopher

Gillie in *Movements in English Literature* (1975) found the impersonality of both poets a characteristically modern feature of their work, John Wain's *Professing Poetry* (1977) identified a self-consciousness in Thomas which he believed to be the hallmark of modern art. Rather surprisingly, Wain also saw him as a Georgian poet, albeit one of the best – 'in respect of things like diction and versification and choice of subject-matter, his aims were their aims'.

Anthony Thwaite in *20th Century Poetry: an Introduction* (1978) calls Thomas's love poetry his 'least successful work', and like Vernon Scannell places him not in the tradition of Eliot and Pound, but with Larkin and Hughes. The poet and critic, P.J. Kavanagh, considered some important contrasts and parallels between Thomas and Richard Jefferies, and Paul Cubieta compared the difficult early careers of Frost and Thomas. In her article 'Rid of this Dream' in the *Anglo-Welsh Review* (No. 62, 1978), Jan Marsh developed the thesis that Thomas hindered his own development as a man and writer by over-idealising the countryside, the starting-point for her book, *Edward Thomas, a Poet for his Country*, published the same year.

The only book entirely devoted to a study of Thomas as poet, Andrew Motion's *The Poetry of Edward Thomas* (1980), relates his work to the middle ground of poetic tradition, between the Georgians and the Modernists. He notes the 'frequent and subtle collisions' in Thomas's verse between the 'unit of the sentence and the unit of the line', and remarks how his poetry reflects a 'mind actually engaged in the act of thinking, rather than offering its concluded thoughts'. It may be added that the placing of Thomas in the 'non-Modernist' tradition has now become a truism and is referred to in passing in Professor Hynes's discussion of the 'Hardy Tradition' in the essay already mentioned (page 19).

Thomas now has his own society – established 1980 – to perpetuate his memory, and Wright's edition of his poetry and prose, Edna Longley's excellent prose selection (both 1981), and *Edward Thomas: a Portrait* by R. G. Thomas in 1985, with much new material about his life, are evidence that for some time to come he will be popular with readers and critics alike.

REVISION QUESTIONS

1. On the evidence of the poems in this selection, how far can Thomas be called a war poet?

2. How would you define and illustrate the quality of sincerity that is often attributed to Thomas's poetry?

3. Discuss the importance of memory in Thomas's poetry.

4. 'It would be the easiest thing in the world to clean it ['Lob'] all up and trim it and have every line straightforward in sound and sense, but it would not really improve it' (Thomas). Do you think Thomas's style is awkward, and how far would you justify it?

5. Is Thomas's poetry too subjective to have universal appeal?

6. 'A verse in which the rhymes are the faintest of echoes, the metre at times scarcely distinguishable' (*Times Literary Supplement*, October 1917). Examine the truth and the implications of these comments on Thomas's style.

7. What evidence would you quote to illustrate Thomas's knowledge and power of observation of the countryside?

8. 'Thomas is as much a poet of exhilaration as of melancholy'. In which role do you think he is the more successful?

9. How effectively do you think Thomas matches form and content?

10. 'A characteristic poem of [Thomas's] has the air of being a random jotting down of chance impressions and sensations' (Leavis). How does he achieve this effect?

11. In what sense is Thomas a patriotic poet?

12. 'One of the ways by which contemporary verse has tried to escape the rhetorical, the abstract, the moralising, to re-cover . . . the accents of direct speech, is to concentrate its attention upon trivial or accidental or commonplace objects' (T. S. Eliot). Consider the implications of Thomas's treatment of the 'trivial'.

13. Thomas's poetry 'often, and perhaps at its best, conveys the impression of a mind thinking about itself' (Jon Silkin). Illustrate and examine this quality of Thomas's writing.

14. Thomas wrote of Richard Jefferies: 'He described this country [Wiltshire] intimately, either for its own sake or because he could not uncover his soul without it'. How does Thomas's response to Nature reflect his own personality?

15. 'He [Thomas] is continually reaching towards an apprehension beyond words' (John Lehmann). Analyse two or three poems in which you find this true of Thomas.

16. How far are Thomas's remarks about Frost's poems also true of his own when he states that they are 'revolutionary because they lack the suggestion of rhetoric, and even at first sight appear to lack . . . poetic intensity'?

17. Define and discuss the 'vein of melancholy and dissatisfaction which runs through Edward Thomas's verse' (R. S. Thomas).

18. How is Thomas's 'scrupulous, self-searching honesty' (R. S. Thomas) reflected in his verse?

FURTHER READING

Poetry

E. Longley (ed.) *Edward Thomas: Poems and Last Poems* (Collins, 1973).

R. G. Thomas (ed.), *Collected Poems of Edward Thomas* (Clarendon Press, 1978; paperback edition, Oxford University Press, 1981).

R. S. Thomas (ed.), *Selected Poems of Edward Thomas* (Faber & Faber, 1964).

Prose

Among the large number of prose works by Thomas, the following may be recommended:

The Heart of England (Oxford University Press, reprint, 1982).

A Literary Pilgrim in England (Oxford University Press, reprint, 1980).

Richard Jefferies (Faber & Faber, reprint, 1978).

Of anthologies of Thomas's prose, the first listed below is particularly useful:

E. Longley (ed.), *A Language Not To Be Betrayed* (Carcanet, 1981).

R. Gant (ed.), *Edward Thomas on the Countryside* (Readers' Union, 1977).

Biography

R. P. Eckert, *Edward Thomas, a Biography and a Bibliography* (Folcroft Library Editions, reprint, 1977).

Eleanor Farjeon, *Edward Thomas: the Last Four Years* (Oxford University Press, 1958).

J. Marsh, *Edward Thomas, a Poet for his Country* (Paul Elek, 1978).

J. Moore, *Life and Letters of Edward Thomas* (Alan Sutton, reprint, 1983).

Helen Thomas, *As It Was and World Without End* (Faber, reprint, 1978).

R. G. Thomas, *Edward Thomas: a Portrait* (Clarendon Press, 1985).

R. G. Thomas (ed.), *Letters from Edward Thomas to Gordon Bottomley* (Oxford University Press, 1968).

Criticism

W. Cooke, *Edward Thomas, a Critical Biography* (Faber & Faber, 1970).

C. Day Lewis, 'The Poetry of Edward Thomas' in *Essays by Divers Hands*, vol. XXVIII, Transactions of the Royal Society of Literature (Oxford University Press, 1956).

A. Motion, *The Poetry of Edward Thomas* (Routledge & Kegan Paul, 1980).

Vernon Scannell, *Edward Thomas* (Writers and their Work, British Council, 1963).

C. H. Sisson, *English Poetry 1900–1950* (Carcanet, 1971, with Postscript, 1981).

C. K. Stead, *The New Poetic* (Penguin, 1969).